Canadian Political Babble

CANADIAN POLITICAL BABBLE

A Cynic's Dictionary of Political Jargon

DAVID OLIVE

Illustrated by Barry Blitt

John Wiley & Sons

Toronto • New York • Chichester • Brisbane • Singapore

John Wiley & Sons Canada Limited
22 Worcester Road
Rexdale, Ontario
M9W 1L1

Canadian Cataloguing in Publication Data
Olive, David, 1957-
Canadian political babble : a cynic's dictionary of political jargon

Includes index.
ISBN 0-471-64078-6

1. Politicians—Canada—Quotations. 2. Politicians—Canada—Humor. 3. Canada—Politics and government—Humor. 4. Canada—Politics and government—Terminology. 5. Canadian wit and humor (English). * I. Title.

FC173.055 1993 081 C93-094777-0
F1026.4.055 1993

Production Credits
Jacket design: Selwyn Simon
Jacket illustrations: Barry Blitt
Text design: Selwyn Simon
Printer: Arcata Graphics Book Group
Printed and bound in the United States
10 9 8 7 6 5 4 3 2 1

To Peter Moore
agent provocateur

Contents

Okay, we've won. What do we do now?

BRIAN MULRONEY, on the night of his re-election as prime minister in 1988

Preface

In politics, novelty is of the essence.

In the Victorian era, only public lynchings competed with political oratory as a source of popular entertainment. The credulity of voters was more easily sustained then, before the advent of investigative journalism and the fishbowl existence with which elected officials must now contend. To win the attention and votes of a modern citizenry distracted by a multitude of mass-media diversions, ambitious office seekers are obliged to make spectacles of themselves in order to attract notice. And this, of course, is their downfall.

Politicians, says *l'Actualité* publisher and veteran political reporter Jean Paré of Montreal, have "made a show out of politics, and therefore have become victims of Rule Number 1 of the genre in the era of zapping: no boredom. If it's boring, zap. Next.

"The only survivors are the hard-working puritans like [Newfoundland premier] Clyde Wells, the pluggers of investment and jobs like [New Brunswick premier] Frank McKenna. Anything that smells of shrewdness, manipulation or hormones is banned. No Ben Johnson. In the stock market of trust, only the rough diamonds of sincerity are accepted. Or of novelty."

Paré suggests that politicians should come with a "best before" date, implying, correctly, that it's the rare politician who enjoys a long shelf life. But there's much more to the politician's life than the task of striving to remain relevant in a rapidly changing world. A surprisingly large number of the basic skills required by today's public figures have remained constant through the ages.

A thick skin is essential, of course. "If you would know the depth of meanness of human nature," noted Sir John A. Macdonald, "you have got to be a prime minister running a general election." A century later, the wily Liberal veteran Jean Chrétien observed that little has changed on that score: "The art of politics," he wrote in his 1985 autobiography, "is learning to walk with your back to the wall, your elbows high, and a smile on your face."

The qualifications for electoral office, apart from *wanting* the job, are annoyingly vague. "To the young members who have just come I would say that for the first six months after you are here you will wonder how you got here," former prime minister John Diefenbaker advised neophyte parliamentarians. "Then after that you will wonder how the rest of the members ever got here." Endurance is an asset, as NDP leader Audrey McLaughlin has noted: "You don't need brains for this job, just physical stamina," she said in the midst of her 1989 leadership campaign. But a clear agenda of what you hope to accomplish is not a prerequisite. Bob Rae, for instance, became premier of Ontario in 1990 not because of what he stood for but because the electorate wasn't excited by the leaders of the two other parties vying to form the government. Hence Rae, by his own admission, was propelled into office without a strong sense of what to do with his new-found power. "I genuinely didn't expect to win the election in 1990," Rae said three years after his surprise victory, "and, in fact, I fully intended to retire after the election. So when I won I was faced with the question, 'What do you do now?'"

Yet elaborate statements of policy can be more dangerous than ducking the issue—hence the temptation to do the latter. "The smart candidate," insisted B.C. premier William Vander Zalm, "avoids detailed policy statements for they rarely help and can do you harm. Your answers should concentrate on style." Attaining a solid grasp of policy is also less fun than cramming for exams, and Liberal leader John Turner said as much to his advisers in 1984 when they presented him with a thick summary of seventy-four key policy issues prior to a planned getaway to Jamaica: "You're trying to wreck my holiday," he complained. "Who cares about this goddam stuff?" Kim Campbell, in her 1993 bid for the Tory leadership, demonstrated an interest in policy but an aversion to be pinned down by it. "[I've had questions] on all my favourite subjects," she said during the leadership campaign. "The really easy ones like capital punishment and abortion and gay rights. I'm in favour of some of those and not of others."

Taking a firm stand, of course, opens the door to embarrassment when a politician inexplicably reverses gears. "Free trade with the United States is simplistic and naïve," said future Tory finance minister Michael Wilson in 1983, trying to distance himself from party leadership rival John Crosbie, who had embraced free trade. "It would only serve to diminish our ability to compete internationally." A few years later, Wilson's boss, Brian Mulroney, explained the duo's dramatic change of heart in aggressively promoting free trade by offering the lame adage that "only donkeys don't change their minds."

If taking potentially unpopular stands isn't a key to political success, a sense of humour most definitely is. "I was offered pot on occasion," admitted Tory strategist Hugh Segal, who briefly flirted with the idea of running for his party's leadership in 1993, "[but] I preferred corned beef." Jean Chrétien went Segal one better. Asked if *he* had experimented with marijuana, Chrétien said, "No. Have you got some?" On being elevated to the post of defence minister in 1993, Kim Campbell issued a wry warning to the press: "Don't mess with me: I've got tanks."

Yet of all the tools in the political arsenal, self-deprecation is probably the most effective, suggesting humility and the common touch. Tommy (T.C.) Douglas, leader of the NDP in the 1960s, seemed to epitomize the politician who doesn't take the game too seriously. "I have often thought that my whole political life—my whole life, as a matter of fact—could be summed up in the words, 'printer, preacher, politician, premier'—or the descent of man." Joe Clark, who emerged as the victor in the 1976 Tory leadership race after finishing a distant third on the first ballot, had no illusions about his towering popularity in the party. "I'm not the greatest," he said in 1977. "I'm the best available." Jean Chrétien similarly made light of his awkward speaking style, saying that "Maurice Chevalier and I worked hard to keep our French accents." Kim Campbell's reaction to the sensation caused by a widely published photograph of her standing with bare shoulders behind her lawyer's robes ignited a short-lived Campbellmania, which Campbell herself was at pains to deflate: "A comparison between Madonna and me is a comparison between a strapless evening gown and a gownless evening strap," she concluded.

This book is not an earnest attempt to explain the intricate machinations of the political game or the factors motivating the players. My hope is simply that in the comments of scores of political figures spanning more that 150 years of Canadian history will be revealed the complex, infuriating, and often amusing characteristics that make up the political personality. The object is less to provide clarity on how the process works—likely an impossible task—but merely to allow those quoted here to reveal insights that make the system at least barely understandable. "If after my talk you are still confused, as you may well be," diplomat and future prime minister Lester Pearson said in concluding a 1956 speech, "I dare to hope that it is at least confusion on a higher plane."

Acknowledgements

I wish to thank the staff of John Wiley & Sons Canada for their assistance in making this book possible; and to acknowledge the generosity of Edwin O'Dacre and the *Globe and Mail* for granting me a leave of absence to complete the work. In particular, I am obliged to cite Grant Swift, Ken Tancock, Kenneth Mucha, and Karen Milner—three fine history teachers and an inspirational editor—as sources of infectious enthusiasm.

A

accessibility *n.* The well-intentioned effort to expose oneself to the slings and arrows of outraged taxpayers who expect their elected employees to make house calls in an era when all but the most conscientious doctors are no longer on call.

Backbenchers in the House of Commons say they are often bored. In big city politics where most citizens have telephones, there is no chance of boredom. Some day, God willing, I will have a home without a telephone.

Calgary mayor GRANT MACEWAN in 1963. MacEwan gradually became accustomed to, and rather fond of, late-night calls from citizens demanding the removal of wasps' nests, the elimination of radio static, and a Beatles concert for his city.

I won the leadership, to most people's surprise, though not to mine. After the convention, Maureen [McTeer] and I went back to our little house, and we were wondering what we had got ourselves into when the phone rang. "Aha," I said. "It must be the prime minister of England or the president of the United States calling to congratulate me." But it was the woman who owned the pizza parlour in Tracadie. She had just lost her liquor licence, and since she couldn't get through to [New Brunswick premier Richard] Hatfield, she wondered if I could help her now that I was leader of the Progressive Conservative Party! It was a rude introduction to what was in store for me.

JOE CLARK in 1983, campaigning to retain the Tory leadership, recalling the short-lived emotional rush he and his wife enjoyed after his 1976 triumph in winning the leadership contest.

adversity *n.* The mother of desperation, or, more sensibly, of philosophical resignation to the inevitably harsh trials of office.

When Fortune empties her chamberpot on your head, smile and say, "We are going to have a summer shower."

Prime Minister JOHN A. MACDONALD

Page One has just one word of advice: duck.

BRIAN MULRONEY in 1993, telling his Tory caucus that he was passing along to his successor Kim Campbell his briefing book on prime ministerial duties

afterlife *n.* The retirement years of a former politician, in which many a scoundrel hopes to be revealed as a saint.

I've achieved my objective. I'm a has-been.

recently retired Ontario premier JOHN ROBARTS in 1971

The surest route to affection and esteem is defeat and retirement.

STEPHEN LEWIS in 1977, upon retiring as Ontario NDP leader

I have come to realize from all the eulogies I have received after I retired that the country did not deserve to have me as prime minister.

former federal Tory leader ROBERT STANFIELD in 1979

You should learn as many trades as you possibly can so that you've always got something to fall back on.

WILLIAM VANDER ZALM, on accepting a starring role in the movie *Sinterklaas Fantasy* while serving as premier of British Columbia

agenda *n.* A thoughtful, comprehensive plan for leading the people to the sunny uplands, which is easily and loudly articulated on the campaign trail and promptly evaporates once its proponents are swept into office.

Okay, we've won. What do we do now?

BRIAN MULRONEY in 1988, moments after learning his party had won re-election

I genuinely didn't expect to win the election in 1990, and, in fact, I fully intended to retire after the election. So when I won I was faced with the question "What do you do now?"

Ontario premier BOB RAE in 1993

alcohol *n.* In earlier times, a principal agent in buying support of apathetic citizens lured to the polling place with promises of free liquor and in steadying the nerves of the luckless souls propelled into office as a result.

Would you move away please? Your breath smells terrible....It smells like water.

JOHN A. MACDONALD, who achieved some of his greatest victories when the spirits moved him

Look here, McGee, *this government can't afford two drunkards — and you've got to stop.*

JOHN A. MACDONALD, having fun at the expense of his friend and cabinet colleague D'Arcy McGee at a political gathering

I know enough of the feeling of this meeting to know that you would rather have John A. drunk than George Brown sober.

JOHN A. MACDONALD, having fun at the expense of strait-laced adversary and fellow Father of Confederation, George Brown.

He is...like many other geniuses, a greater friend of the bottle than the bottle is to him.

WILLIAM LYON MACKENZIE, first mayor of Toronto and leader of the Upper Canada rebellion of 1837, on the drinking habits of an acquaintance

One of the interesting things about this job is that you are precluded from doing a lot of things, obviously. You know, you can't go on a good pub crawl any more.

newly elected Prime Minister BRIAN MULRONEY in 1985, reflecting on the downside of holding a high political office

ambiguity *n.* The protective coloration of the political animal, whose survival instincts include a keen sense that a predator's favourite feast is the misguided clarity of its prey.

Not necessarily conscription, but conscription if necessary.

Prime Minister MACKENZIE KING unveiling his conscription policy during the Second World War

Never let your "on the one hand" know what your "on the other hand" is doing....Do nothing by halves which can be done by quarters.

poet F.R. SCOTT in 1957, on the style of Mackenzie King

You know, we used to say: "With an 'if' here and an 'if' there, you can put Paris in a bottle."

economist and politician ERIC KIERANS on the powerful impact of subtle manipulations of language when crafting legislation

The budget is stimulative. It is less stimulative than if it had been more, but it is more than if it had been less.

Prime Minister PIERRE TRUDEAU in 1982

[I've had questions] on all my favourite subjects. The really easy ones like capital punishment and abortion and gay rights. I'm in favour of some of those things and not of others.

Tory leadership hopeful KIM CAMPBELL in 1993, donning the shroud of constructive ambiguity

ambition *n.* The triumph of ego over humility.

I can't waste any time on you, Prime Minister, I must get about my work.

JOHN DIEFENBAKER, a Prince Albert, Saskatchewan, newsboy, during a chance meeting with local MP and prime minister, Wilfrid Laurier, as recalled by Laurier. During his own tenure as prime minister, Diefenbaker was fond of saying, "As Prince Albert goes, so goes the nation"—an observation prompted in part by the riding's distinction of having been represented by no fewer than three prime ministers: Laurier, Mackenzie King, and Dief.

I am king of my own little island, and that's all I've ever wanted to be.

JOEY SMALLWOOD, premier of Newfoundland, when asked by Liberal Party officials in 1959 to consider a run at the federal party leadership

One thing's for sure, Joe: if you don't run, you won't win.

friendly advice from Liberal cabinet minister JEAN CHRÉTIEN to rookie MP Joe Clark, who doubted his chances of winning the 1976 Tory leadership contest and wondered if he should even bother trying

I know, the Queen Mother was telling me that just the other day.

BRIAN MULRONEY, backroom Tory strategist,
responding to a friend's advice that he curb
his habit of incessant name-dropping

Because it's there....If you're in business, you want to become president of the company; if you're in politics, you want to become leader.

Tory leadership hopeful JOHN CROSBIE in 1983,
explaining what motivated his candidacy

arrogance *n.* The least avoidable outcome of electoral success.

Do you think I want a lot of long-haired professors telling me what to do? If I can't run this country, I will get out.

Prime Minister R.B. BENNETT in 1931. Making good
on his promise, upon being defeated in 1935, Bennett
moved to Britain, where he spent
the rest of his life.

You and all the other damn Rhodes scholars! Get the hell out of here!

Liberal cabinet minister C.D. HOWE dismissing
a group of professors from his office

The more I see of Premier Lesage, the more I appreciate the humility of General de Gaulle.

Newfoundland premier JOEY SMALLWOOD on the imperious nature of Jean Lesage, premier of Quebec from 1960 to 1966, compared to that of French president Charles de Gaulle

When I see Mulroney, I realize how humble was Charles de Gaulle. When I see Kim Campbell, I realize how humble is Brian Mulroney.

Liberal leader JEAN CHRÉTIEN in 1993, on his Tory counterpart, Kim Campbell

Well, why should I sell the Canadian farmers' wheat?

Prime Minister PIERRE TRUDEAU in 1968 at a Liberal Party meeting in Winnipeg

Tell him to move to Regina.

PIERRE TRUDEAU in 1974 , to a Liberal organizer who fretted that he didn't know what to tell a friend who couldn't afford to buy a house in a Toronto suburb due to inflation and soaring real estate prices

In any case, it's only puritans from outside Quebec who worry about little things like that.

Quebec premier ROBERT BOURASSA in 1975, on revelations of corruption in government and the construction industry. One year later, Bourassa's government was defeated by the Parti Québécois.

I was elected to run New Brunswick. No one said I had to live *there.*

New Brunswick premier RICHARD HATFIELD, brushing off criticism about his frequent getaways to New York and Paris

We are living in an unsatisfied society. Half the world today is unhappy because it doesn't have enough food to eat. The other half is unhappy because the garbage pickers are on strike, or there is too much pollution in the air, or, Christ, they have only three television stations instead of five. The richest people beef even worse. You know, the worst bitchers are bankers.

PIERRE TRUDEAU, prime minister and the rich inheritor of his father's oil-company fortune, beefing about people who beef in 1976

The reason you get into politics is because you don't want to be governed by people who are less good than yourself.

PIERRE TRUDEAU in 1978

When there is too much sun, they complain. When there is too much rain, they complain. A farmer is a complainer.

PIERRE TRUDEAU on the eve of his 1979 electoral defeat

The sovereign would have to ask me three times on bended knee.

PIERRE TRUDEAU's response in 1979 to caucus colleagues who asked him to reverse his decision to quit the Liberal Party leadership

I only ran for mayor because the others were dodos.

Toronto mayor JOHN SEWELL in 1980, the year of his humbling defeat after serving only one term

I do have an I.Q. in the three digits, and I'm prepared to stand up in the House and discuss these things.

KIM CAMPBELL, member of the B.C. legislature in 1987-88, in parliamentary debate

[This bill] is very complex because clearly [the Opposition members] don't understand it. I suspect some of them haven't read it; I suspect after three pages their lips get tired.

B.C. MLA KIM CAMPBELL in parliamentary debate

I'm sorry Honourable Member. Are words of two syllables a little too difficult for you to understand?

B.C. MLA KIM CAMPBELL in parliamentary debate

Every time I look...at the other side of the House...I just feel better and better.

Prime Minister BRIAN MULRONEY in 1993, hinting that the sub-par calibre of his likely opponents in a future election was a strong indication that he intended to hang around and attempt to lead his party to victory once again

With a leader like this, my expectation is that the Triple Crown is just around the corner.

BRIAN MULRONEY in 1993, mocking Liberal leader Jean Chrétien's ability to prevent Mulroney from winning a third straight majority in the next election

The thing that infuriates me is apathy. People who boast about how they've never been involved in a political party. Who do they think is working to keep this society intact so they can have the luxury of sitting back and being such condescending SOBs? To hell with them.

Tory leadership hopeful KIM CAMPBELL in a 1993 interview with Peter C. Newman

B

backbencher *n.* The pawns of parliamentary politics, whose subservience to their party's leadership is rewarded with memberships on obscure subcommittees and the occasional taxpayer-funded fact-finding junket to Outer Nowhere.

I think we should encourage members of the Opposition to leave. Every time they do, the I.Q. of this House rises considerably. The best place in which to talk, if they want a forum, is, of course, Parliament. When they get home, when they get out of Parliament, when they are fifty yards from Parliament Hill, they are no longer Honourable Members, they are just nobodies, Mr. Speaker.

Prime Minister PIERRE TRUDEAU in 1969, in an address to Parliament only four years after first being elected to the House, where he suffered the anonymity of being a backbencher for a remarkably brief time before being elevated to a cabinet post

I sit so goddam far back they don't even turn on the mike when I speak.

FRANK DREA, erstwhile high-profile journalist turned Tory backbencher in the Ontario government, in 1972. Drea's patience was rewarded with a cabinet posting in 1977.

bathos *n.* The deployment of self-pity as a device to cover a multitude of sins.

I see our CBC friends decided old Mulroney's problems with the Senate were more important than the San Francisco earthquake last week. Did you see that?

BRIAN MULRONEY seeking the support of fellow MPs at a weekly caucus session in 1989

I think they are looking at Christmas dinner and I'm the turkey.

GORDON WILSON in 1993 after stepping down as B.C. Liberal Party leader, citing the distraction of a looming acrimonious separation from his wife, who he said had hired a "rabidly feminist lawyer" to represent her. Wilson's forced ouster from the party's top spot was owed mostly to his erratic behaviour and the controversy over his installing as the party's house leader a woman with whom he was widely believed to be having an affair.

biculturalism *n.* Ill-fated attempt to recognize the French-English duality of Canada by showering unwanted largesse on francophones and unwanted bilingually labelled cereal boxes on anglophones, a program whose demonstrated success spawned the still more ambitious policy of multiculturalism, in which taxpayer funds were expended to buy the political support of dozens of nationalities.

Biculture? What breed of bull is that? I've heard of agriculture and horticulture, even floriculture and aviculture. But biculture?

EUGENE WHELAN, future agriculture minister in the

Trudeau government, discussing the Royal Commission on Bilingualism and Biculturalism with his Liberal caucus colleagues in 1965

big leagues *n.* The federal and provincial arenas, political forums where style triumphs over substance, in contrast to school boards, where members are expected to do something meaningful—like banning the occasional book and jacking up property taxes without anyone noticing. In Canada, hockey is appropriately the big-league sport of choice in crafting political metaphors.

The art of politics is learning to walk with your back to the wall, your elbows high, and a smile on your face.

former Liberal MP JEAN CHRÉTIEN in his 1985 autobiography *Straight from the Heart*

In politics, they play a lot more dirty than in hockey.

Montreal Canadiens hero GUY LAFLEUR in 1992, on the acrimony he encountered while campaigning for the Yes side in the referendum on the Charlottetown constitutional accord

If you play peewee hockey, you sometimes think it would be

nice to get into the NHL, until they discover you don't skate very fast.

Tory strategist and Montreal Canadiens devotee HUGH SEGAL in 1993, briefly considering and quickly rejecting a bid for the leadership of his party. "Too bad about Hugh Segal and his three-day flirtation with the race," Mordecai Richler wrote in the June 1993 issue of *Saturday Night* magazine. "I first suspected that Segal, *rara avis*, a Tory of wit and intelligence, withdrew because he grasped that, campaigning in Don Getty's big-sky country, he would have been obliged to explain his punch lines." (Former pro football player Getty was Alberta premier in the 1980s and 1990s.)

bilingualism *n.* The late 20th-century requirement that political candidates demonstrate a polished ability to equivocate and prevaricate in both official languages.

For the benefit of those who are not bilingual, I will now continue in English.

Prime Minister JOHN DIEFENBAKER

I haven't practised my French. It's just that you are starting to understand it.

John Diefenbaker in 1965, responding to a reporter who noted that his notoriously awkward way with the other official language seemed to have improved of late

What really upsets me about those "Let the Eastern Bastards Freeze in the Dark" stickers is that they weren't bilingual.

Liberal cabinet minister Bryce Mackasey in 1976, speaking in Regina at a time when western Canadian antipathy towards Central Canada had reached an all-time high

Would you be here tonight to listen to a French Canadian talking to you through a translator?

Joe Clark in 1983, campaigning against rival Tory leadership hopeful John Crosbie, whose chief liability was an almost determined inability to communicate in French

It is better to be honest and sincere in one language than a twister, a trickster, and a twit in two.

John Crosbie campaigning for the Tory leadership in 1983, defending his unilingual status

Canada has two official languages and I don't speak none of them.

retired Liberal MP EUGENE WHELAN in his 1986 autobiography, *Whelan: The Man in the Green Stetson*

The federal government has responded to Quebec nationalism by introducing bilingual menus in northern Saskatchewan.

former Quebec premier and Parti Québécois leader PIERRE-MARC JOHNSON in 1988

[We attended] a Reform Party fundraising dinner to check out the competition. But when one of us ordered quiche lorraine, we were thrown out for speaking French.

MARTY WILLIAMS and DOUGLAS POWELL, candidate and campaign manager, respectively, for the Rhinoceros Party in the Ontario riding of Guelph-Wellington, in 1991

I can get very emotional in French.

Tory leadership candidate JOHN LONG in 1993, asserting his less-than-perfect grasp of French would not hurt him in a French-only TV debate among leadership rivals

boast *n.* A diversionary tactic whose impact is directly proportionate to the incredulity it inspires.

A very substantial success compared to anything this country has seen in recent memory.

newly elected Prime Minister BRIAN MULRONEY in 1985, claiming credit for creating 271,000 jobs in the eight months since his election. In fact, the eight-month record was held by the previous Trudeau regime: 316,000 jobs were created in 1982-83. The Mulroney boast helped distract media attention from the huge volume of patronage appointments his government was making.

Canada is Number 1, not Number 14 or Number 41. Number 1. Not Bad. Not bad for a guy from Baie-Comeau.

Prime Minister BRIAN MULRONEY in 1992, referring to Canada's ranking in a United Nations quality-of-life survey in a vain attempt to shift the public's focus away from his government's inexpert handling of an economy which was suffering its worst downturn since the Depression

budget *n.* The government's spending plans and revenue receipts for the year to come, vying with the better Harlequin volumes as a masterwork of inflated expectations and happy outcomes.

I could give no better description of this budget than to use the words of Abraham Lincoln when, in 1858, he described a budget by saying it "was as thin as the homeopathic soup that was made by boiling the shadow of a pigeon that had starved to death."

Tory Opposition MP JOHN DIEFENBAKER in 1970, describing a Trudeau government budget

When it comes to budget cuts, everyone wants to go to Heaven, but nobody wants to die.

attributed to JEAN CHRÉTIEN in 1978 when he was federal finance minister

You see this here, this little piece of paper cost you $200 million. Yup, that's the price you had to pay when Marc Lalonde became the first Canadian politician ever caught in the act of leaking.

JOHN CROSBIE, campaigning for the Tory leadership in 1983, referring to federal finance minister

Lalonde's gaffe in inadvertently exposing budget documents to a TV crew prior to formally making them public in Parliament, which required a revision—in this case a $200 million increase in public spending—to maintain the semblance of budget secrecy

[He was forced to] throw off this reform and then that one until he was left naked as a newt. He became the Gypsy Rose Lee of Canadian politics.

JOHN CROSBIE, campaigning for the Tory leadership in 1983, referring to Liberal finance minister Allan MacEachen's staged retreat from provisions of his disastrous "reform" budget of 1981

No matter how we define the term, Canada has an acute shortage of rich people.

Tory finance minister MICHAEL WILSON in 1985, defending his decision not to raise taxes on the wealthy

bureaucracy *n.* The civil servants who do a government's heavy lifting and, in return for job security, stoically accept their role as chief scapegoat for politicians seeking to deflect attention from their own misadventures.

A pink slip and a pair of running shoes.

BRIAN MULRONEY campaigning for the Tory leadership in 1983, describing what his government would hand any bureaucrat who blocked job-creating investment

You go up to Ottawa to see one of those bureaucrats in their offices, which are usually larger than your factory, and you don't know if they will talk to you or send you out for coffee.

Tory leader BRIAN MULRONEY campaigning for prime minister in 1984, playing to the anti-government sentiments of a business audience

C

cabinet *n.* The ruling party's supreme decision-making body. The words of its members are final—except when they conflict with the directives issued by the relatives, cronies, and paid personal advisers of the prime minister or premier, who alone determines who shall be selected for membership.

A nest of traitors.

Sir MACKENZIE BOWELL, fifth prime minister of Canada, in 1896, on learning that half the members of his own cabinet had resigned over his handling of the issue of the use of the French language in Manitoba schools. Within four months of the crisis, Bowell joined the "traitors" by resigning himself.

Like any cabinet maker, I do the best I can with the lumber you furnish me.

Prime Minister JOHN A. MACDONALD to a farmer who had complained, "Send me better men to deal with, and I will be a better man."

I took you out of the gutter. Keep your mouth shut, or I'll put you back where I found you!

Quebec premier MAURICE DUPLESSIS to a renegade cabinet minister

I've got all my enemies in the cabinet where I can keep an eye on them.

attributed to JOHN DIEFENBAKER in 1959, when he was prime minister

There are poor people in the cabinet, and there are certainly people in the cabinet that are getting poorer, I can tell you that.

PIERRE TRUDEAU in 1968, a few months after becoming prime minister

Our cabinet is always unanimous—except when we disagree.

B.C. premier WILLIAM VANDER ZALM

Canada-U.K. relations *n.* An increasingly distant relationship between a child no longer much interested in keeping in touch with a parent, and a parent who encourages the trend, ever confident of its vast superiority to the child in every respect.

We have found that our Canadian independence is quite compatible with our dependence as a colony.

Prime Minister WILFRID LAURIER in 1904

I don't even know what street Britain is on.

Canadian political commentator KATHERINE WESTCOTT in 1993, in a twist on Al Capone's similar observation about Canada

Canada-U.S. relations *n.* Big Brother isn't watching you, but he's paying the bills: the increasingly close relationship between a child and its older, wiser, and richer sibling, who knows only that the child is on a hunting trip somewhere north of Montana.

These Yankee politicians are the lowest race of thieves in existence.

Canadian justice minister JOHN THOMPSON expressing frustration after meeting with his U.S. negotiating counterparts over a dispute about fishing rights in the 1880s

The last time Prime Minister Trudeau came to our country he said that being a neighbour to the United States was like sleeping with an elephant—that you could very quickly detect every twitch or grunt. Well, the elephants are gone. The donkeys are here. And the donkeys are much more companionable beasts, I think.

U.S. president JIMMY CARTER in 1977, greeting Prime Minister Pierre Trudeau at the White House with a reference to a changing of the guard from a Republican administration (symbolized by the elephant) to a Democratic one (donkey)

This land is your land, this land is my land,
From California to Vancouver Island.

A PICK-UP BAND at a Tory picnic in Toronto during Brian Mulroney's first campaign for prime minister in 1984 keeps faith with the U.S., rather than the Canadian, version of the classic tune—whose Canadian lyrics read, "From Bona Vista to Vancouver Island."

The U.S. is our greatest friend, neighbour and ally. Now, that relationship doesn't suggest any degree of compliance or servility. The fact of the matter is, if I were the president I would wake up every morning and say, "Thank God for Canada. Now, what can I do for Canada?"

Prime Minister BRIAN MULRONEY in a post-election interview with *Time* in 1984

So my family became the first Canadian family to benefit directly from American foreign aid.

Newly elected prime minister BRIAN MULRONEY in 1984, addressing the Economic Club of New York, seeing virtue in depicting for the benefit of a foreign audience Canada's abject reliance on foreign investment, which Mulroney knew first-hand, he explained, having received $50 each time he was called forward as a young boy in his native Baie-Comeau to sing "Dearie" for a visiting Colonel McCormick of Chicago, owner of the *Chicago Tribune* and its paper mill in Mulroney's home town.

The general impression you get is that our prime minister invited his boss home for dinner.

former Liberal cabinet minister ERIC KIERANS in 1985, on that year's summit between Brian Mulroney and

visiting U.S. president Ronald Reagan at the
so-called Shamrock Summit in Quebec City

Some tinpot dictator can command infinitely more attention in the United States and in Congress than can a tremendous ally and friend like Canada.

Prime Minister BRIAN MULRONEY in a U.S.
television interview in 1986

There is anti-Americanism in Canada, but not enough to get you elected dogcatcher.

Prime Minister BRIAN MULRONEY in 1988. The remark seemed to remind the commentators of the degree to which all things American influenced Mulroney: in Canada, dogcatchers are appointed, not elected.

candour *n.* A device to be employed when all others have failed.

Gentlemen, we all must realize that neither side has any monopoly on sons of bitches.

federal cabinet minister C.D. HOWE, kicking off a difficult negotiating session over a shipping dispute in Washington, D.C.

What is Social Credit? Elect me and I'll find out.

campaign slogan of MARGARET MURRAY, newspaper publisher and Socred candidate in the early 1950s

We know people are saying, "You [MPs] are a bunch of clowns," and they're right—we are a bunch of clowns and I think it's time for us to stop.

Liberal MP JOHN EVANS in 1982

There are no skeletons in my closet—there are too many clothes.

MARILYN LASTMAN, candidate for city council in the Toronto suburb of North York and wife of North York mayor and retail magnate Mel Lastman, in 1988. Mr. Lastman was re-elected, but his wife did not win a council seat.

I think the results stink.

B.C. premier RITA JOHNSTON in 1991, dispensing with the usual election-night chin-up tact in conceding defeat as her government fell to the Opposition NDP led by Michael Harcourt

It's hard to pin down precise dates on these things.

FLOYD LAUGHREN, finance minister of the NDP government of Ontario, in 1992, responding to a reporter's question, "When did your government lose its grip on reality?"

On top of a timber outlook near Port Alberni.

Tory leadership hopeful KIM CAMPBELL in 1993, responding without hesitation to journalist Peter C. Newman's query at the buffet table in the staid main dining room of Victoria's Empress hotel: "So where were you conceived?"

I don't know what I'm doing but I'm good at it.

message on a pin offered to Tory leadership candidate KIM CAMPBELL in 1993, which she gamely attached to her blouse next to her trademark "KC" brooch

career-eliminating comment *n.* A non-retractable, inexplicable reputation-endangering verbal miscue.

I cannot talk to the Chinese people in their own language either....I can't talk to the German people in their own language. Does that mean there should be no relationships between China and Canada or Canada and Germany, or whatever?...There are many different languages.

JOHN CROSBIE torpedos his chances of winning the Tory leadership contest in 1983, accosting Montreal reporters who persisted with questions about how his inability to speak French disqualified him from a leading national party. His remarks ignited a *cause célèbre*: typical media coverage of his comments was *Le Journal de Montréal*'s headline, "For Crosbie, French Is Not More Important Than Chinese or German."

Short-term pain for long-term gain.

JOHN CROSBIE, finance minister in the short-lived Tory government of Joe Clark, in 1979, unveiling a reviled austerity budget that included an 18 percent-per-gallon boost in the excise tax on gasoline. Within a few weeks, the Opposition Liberals succeeded in using Crosbie's promise of "short-term pain" to defeat Clark's government, and then proceeded to implement their own gas-tax increase.

And I said that's the day that I'm going to roll all the dice. It's the only way to handle it.

Prime Minister BRIAN MULRONEY in a June 12, 1990, interview with the *Globe and Mail*, in which he explained his strategy for manipulating the premiers into signing onto the Meech Lake constitutional accord. Mulroney's premature boasting about his negotiating skills helped galvanize popular distrust of the accord, which died later that month when it failed to achieve ratification in the legislatures of Manitoba and Newfoundland. Thereafter, Mulroney was haunted by the "roll the dice" expression, which was applied to his every political misstep, past and present.

caucus *n.* A club consisting of legislature members ostensibly hailing from the same political party and whose loyalty to the leader diminishes and capacity for rebellious mischief increases in direct proportion to the party's performance in public-opinion polls.

What is the difference between the Conservative caucus and a porcupine? Well, you see, a porcupine has all its pricks on the outside.

deposed Conservative leader JOHN DIEFENBAKER

Please wait for my punch lines. I don't want this spontaneous applause—it's not caucus.

JOE CLARK speaking to an Edmonton audience that cheered him too quickly, in a self-deprecating reference to the constant second-guessing from his caucus colleagues, who doubted his leadership abilities after his government was toppled in 1980

I can't hold the party together by blaming others, but it's extremely annoying that the people who were the architects of my problems then exploited the wounds in my carcass.

JOE CLARK campaigning to retain the Tory leadership in 1983, referring to caucus backstabbers whose actions helped create the impression of Clark's "ineffectiveness," which they now cited as a reason for Clark to be dumped

I can see the headlines after the next election: "Liberals Sweep to Victory—Liberal Caucus Demands Recount."

Liberal leader JOHN TURNER in 1988, on the persistent unhappiness with his stewardship of the party within his own ranks

I'm a child of this party. I saw too many leaders go down the chute because they lost control of their caucus. I was resolved it would not happen to me.

BRIAN MULRONEY on the eve of retirement in 1993, on his strategy for suppressing internal dissent while serving as Tory leader

charismatically challenged *adj.* Describes a condition in which an elected official's chronic inability to make a lasting favourable impression—or *any* impression—is his or her most distinctive trait.

What is the totality of your land?

Tory leader JOE CLARK struggles to make small talk with a foreign dignitary during a 1979 world tour.

No shirt is too young to be stuffed.

broadcaster LARRY ZOLF on the Tories' young leader Joe Clark

Bland works.

sage advice on how to stay out of trouble from Bland Brampton (Ontario) BILLY DAVIS, a.k.a. William G. Davis, winner of four straight elections as premier of Ontario, beginning in the early 1970s. "He did nothing in particular," Kim Campbell has said in assessing Davis's political record. "I think that could characterize Bill Davis's approach to government."

I only take my shirt off for Lois Lane.

Tory finance minister MICHAEL WILSON, responding to the question, "When are you going to take off your Clark Kent disguise and become Superman?"—an invitation to disprove the widespread assumption that there was no secret life lurking behind Wilson's actuarial demeanour

My great fear was that I might become know as the candidate of substance without charisma.

Tory leadership hopeful KIM CAMPBELL in 1993, announcing her candidacy and harking back to her memorable dig at her rival for the B.C. Socred leadership, William Vander Zalm, of whom she said in 1986 that "charisma without substance is a dangerous thing"

Hey, no, not that. Maybe more like the Beatles or Elvis Presley.

Liberal leader JEAN CHRÉTIEN in 1993, insisting during an appearance on rock-video network MuchMusic that he's not a Lawrence Welk kind of guy

chauvinism, civic *n.* My city, right or wrong.

As long as we keep a good balance between prayer and sinning, I know my city is not going to sink into wickedness.

Montreal mayor CAMILLIEN HOUDE

I'll be happy to come back to Toronto to kick your balls off any time you want.

Montreal mayor CAMILLIEN HOUDE in 1946, after attending the ceremonial kick-off at a Grey Cup game in Toronto

It is going to be one hell of a city once it's finally uncrated.

Calgary mayor RALPH KLEIN in 1982, on the hectic building boom underway in his town

Edmonton isn't exactly the end of the world, but you can see it from there.

Calgary mayor RALPH KLEIN

chauvinism, national *n.* My country, right or wrong.

[Canada is more than] moose, mountains, and Mounties.

federal tourism minister TOM MCMILLAN in 1985

chauvinism, regional *n.* My province, right or wrong.

Poor, bald rock.

Premier JOEY SMALLWOOD's description of Newfoundland

Newfoundland: a piece of rock entirely surrounded by fog.

Premier JOEY SMALLWOOD in 1968

civil liberties *n.* The right to freedom of expression, the most unseemly display of which is exhibited during legislative debates.

I knew he would never marry Barbra Streisand or any American girl. I can recall him saying the States has no place in the bedrooms of the nation.

Tory leader ROBERT STANFIELD in 1971, on hearing about Prime Minister Pierre Trudeau's wedding plans. In a 1967 interview, then-justice minister Trudeau commented on his proposed changes to the Criminal Code, saying, "There's no place for the state in the bedrooms of the nation." Two years later, fending off questions about his rumoured liaisons with Eva Rittinghausen, Trudeau said, "I think you once agreed when I said that the state had no place in the bedrooms of the nation. I think we could even say that the country has no place in the bedrooms of the state, and certainly not the press anyhow." Streisand, a frequent Trudeau date who shared his liberal ideology, did not think much of the food at 24 Sussex Drive, the prime minister's official residence in Ottawa, announcing her suspicions about the dessert during a meal there by saying, "This **is** Sara Lee!"

It is all too easy, should disturbances erupt, to crush [civil liberties] in the name of law and order. We must never forget that in the long run, a democracy is judged by the way the majority treats the minority. Louis Riel's battle is not yet won.

Prime Minister PIERRE TRUDEAU in 1969, paying homage to the leader of the Red River Rebellion

It is more important to maintain law and order than to worry about those whose knees tremble at the sight of the army.

Prime Minister PIERRE TRUDEAU in 1970, justifying the suppression of civil liberties during the FLQ crisis

confrontation *n.* The clash of theatrical rhetoric and petty obstinance that characterizes most political activity.

There was a time when we were younger and things were better, when many Canadians, I think, looked upon [Prime Minister Pierre] Trudeau's penchant for confrontation as a kind of political theatre. Well, we may still find that more than four hours of Napoleon versus Europe makes a good movie, but we know now that more than fourteen years of Mr. Trudeau versus everyone else makes lousy government.

Tory leader BRIAN MULRONEY on the campaign trail in 1984, girding up for confrontations of his own with premiers, union leaders, economic nationalists, feminists, poverty and child-care advocates, the media....

consensus *n.* A happy meeting of minds, usually achievable only when the minds in question happen for the moment to be asleep.

The only place in this world that you find unanimity is in the graveyard.

Quebec premier MAURICE DUPLESSIS

The committee will be composed of open-minded people who agree with me.

ED MCKITKA, mayor of Surrey, British Columbia, announcing a new municipal committee to censor art shows

I come from a history of "I don't know, what do you think?"

NDP leader AUDREY MCLAUGHLIN in 1990, on her consensual leadership style, which, while admirable, encouraged open splits among partisans on Quebec nationalism, the austerity program of the party's Ontario counterpart, and other issues, and which helped drag down the party's popularity

Conservative Party *n.* Formerly the party opposed to free trade, or "reciprocity," with the United States, which held power—infrequently—when the Natural Governing Party, the Liberals, was on sabbatical. Currently the party that supports free trade with the United States, to the benefit of the Liberals, who now oppose free trade—a sign that voters must now look for consistency to the Rhinoceros Party, which has never wavered from its pledge to repeal the laws of gravity.

A Liberal is a Liberal because he likes something or somebody; a Tory is a Tory because he hates somebody or something.

Liberal cabinet minister ERNEST LAPOINTE in 1919

I don't trust this new bunch.

C.D. HOWE, former Liberal cabinet minister, upon the defeat of the government of which he had been a top minister, instructing his broker to sell most of his stocks

Why, I used to be a Tory when I was young and uninformed. I was a Tory until I could stand no more. They're all lawyers—there's nothing wrong with lawyers, but there are just too many of them. They spend all their time changing commas, changing the constitution, and changing their leaders.

W.A.C. BENNETT, former B.C. premier, in 1973

contempt *n.* The proper sentiment of partisans towards their leader who is sagging in popular appeal.

If I walked on water, people would say I couldn't swim.

Liberal leader JOHN TURNER on misgivings about his abilities expressed by fellow Liberals

contrition *n.* A bid for redemption when the fruits of arrogance begin falling from the tree.

I'll tell you one thing that's certain. From now on, no more philosopher king.

a chastened PIERRE TRUDEAU after the near-defeat of his government in 1972, vowing to shed his aloof style. Trudeau's easy acquaintance with philosophical writings was part of his electoral appeal in 1967, when he was asked, "How badly do you want to be prime minister," and he responded, "Not very badly. But I can give you another quotation, from Plato—that men who want very badly to head the country shouldn't be trusted."

conversion *n.* The proper act of the politician whose highly principled, firmly held belief isn't selling with the voters.

The philosophy of the Liberal Party is very simple—say anything, think anything, or better still, do not think at all, but put us in power because it is we who can govern you best.

journalist PIERRE TRUDEAU in 1963. Five years later, Trudeau was elected leader of the Liberal Party, which he promptly led to a sweeping electoral victory.

I don't want to be a public figure, I've got work to do.

BOB BLAIR, CEO of Calgary-based Nova Corp., in 1978. In 1993, Blair had retired from Nova and accepted a Liberal Party nomination in order to seek election to the House of Commons.

I have said on several occasions, but never face-to-face to him, that he has surely been the most remarkable Canadian of his generation.

Liberal leadership hopeful JOHN TURNER paying homage to Pierre Trudeau at the party's 1984 convention, where he sought to replace Trudeau, whom he had bad-mouthed before and after serving in his government in the 1970s. "Holy Christ," a supporter of Turner leadership rival Jean Chrétien said, "if he can say that, he can say anything. I can't believe it."

If a politician doesn't get at least one free meal a day, that day is a total loss.

former Ontario premier WILLIAM DAVIS presiding at an awards banquet in 1993. While premier, Davis was fond of explaining his government's austerity measures by invoking the tired adage, "There is no such thing as a free lunch."

Only donkeys don't change their minds.

Prime Minister BRIAN MULRONEY in 1988, on his about-face on free trade

corruption *n.* A rare lapse from the Olympian standards of honesty by which government activity is conducted.

There is a clear distinction between being a Liberal contractor and being dishonest.

Quebec premier ROBERT BOURASSA, besieged by scandal, in 1973

culture *n.* In America, any entertainment that can command a paying audience. In Canada, government-funded expressions of national identity.

Two cans of paint, and two rollers and about ten minutes would do the trick.

Tory MP FELIX HOLTMANN, chairman of the Commons culture and communications committee, in 1990, describing how little work likely went into the creation of U.S. artist Barnett Newman's abstract painting *Voice of Fire*, whose purchase by the National Gallery of Canada for $1.76 million was criticized by Holtmann and other MPs. During his tenure on the culture committee, Holtmann also mused that CBC Radio should do away with broadcasts of Beethoven and other "foreign music" and interrupt its program schedule with commercials.

So really, all of the cultural emphasis for Canadian publishing means you're talking 95 percent of people subsidizing the other 5 percent. Does it contribute to national unity? Possibly. But not that much.

Tory MP Charles Cook in 1991, arguing for a reduction in federal subsidies to the Canadian book publishing industry. By Cook's calculation, only 10 percent of Canadians read books—or maybe only 5 percent, after subtracting romances, mysteries, light fiction, and bestsellers. Allowing that he was a little better-read than the average person, Cook said he read three titles each week, but preferred foreign bestselling authors Frederick Forsyth and Tom Clancy to local writers. "Not too much Canadian stuff" found its way onto Cook's reading list, "because it's just not good enough."

D

debate *n.* Heated discussion that mimics bar-room exchanges save that the former is conducted according to Roberts' Rules of Order.

Once a louse, always a louse.

Liberal cabinet minister C.D. HOWE, in a retort to Tory heckler Donald Fleming, who responded, "You should know."

Are we having a debate?...I do not think this should be allowed to degenerate into a debate.

C.D. HOWE, speaking in Parliament

I feel they're frittering away hours in meaningless haranguing when they should be getting important things accomplished.

MARYON PEARSON, wife of Liberal leader Lester Pearson, on the quality of parliamentary debate

Fuddle duddle.

PIERRE TRUDEAU in 1971, insisting this, and not the f-word, is what he had said in parliamentary debate

Temper? I have no temper....I've never lost my temper. Righteous indignation is another thing!

W.A.C. BENNETT, premier of British Columbia from 1952 to 1972

If the minister of finance had the courage and the conviction of a garrotted gerbil, he would resign tomorrow. He is worse than a castrated lemming today—he is a garrotted gerbil.

Tory finance critic JOHN CROSBIE in 1980, referring to Liberal finance minister Allan MacEachen

Shut up, Sambo.

attributed to Alberta MP JACK SHIELDS, apparently directed at the House of Commons' only black member, Howard McCurdy, in 1991. Shields denied making the remark, but apologized for unspecified comments.

Fucking bastard.

attributed to Prime Minister BRIAN MULRONEY in 1991, referring to an opposition member in parliamentary debate

[He is] the crappiest Speaker.

Alberta Liberal leader NICK TAYLOR in 1991, attacking legislative speaker David Carter. By 1993, Carter, a former Anglican church dean who had grown weary of unparliamentary language, had extended to 172 the number of words and phrases he banned from use in the legislature, including ass, crap, camouflage, dumb, flunky, goosed, idiot, quacking, scuzzball, slippery Larry, weasel, and witch hunt. Many of the outlawed terms, including boondocks, buddy, herd, and cowbell are innocuous, and no one save Carter seems to know why they're on the verboten list. "Cowbell" appears to have joined the list because in 1989 Taylor called a heckler a "cowbell...[with] the longest tongue and emptiest head." Unparliamentary language, defined as utterances that disrupt the legislature or bring it into disrepute, date back to the first phrase to be banned, in 1875, when one British MP called another a "pugilist and political bully." In Canada, the House of Commons banned "blatherskite" in 1890; a blatherskite is someone who is longwinded and silly. Alberta's speaker seems to take matters to extremes. When an Opposition MLA attacked a government minister as someone who "acts like a mouse, squeaks like a mouse and is a mouse," Carter banned the whole sentence, where it joined other forbidden phrases such as "fat, wingless ducks" in a "forum of drunken first impressions." Carter applies the ban selectively; he himself has labelled the Opposition as "thin-skinned" and in an exchange with NDP leader Pam Barrett said his own voice wasn't as "squeaky" as hers.

defence, national *n.* Except in wartime, a function largely delegated to the Pentagon, excepting the fleet of skiffs used to defend a perimeter of coastlines more extensive than that of any nation.

Canada doesn't make anything that goes bang.

former defence minister BARNEY DANSON, regretting the focus of Canada's arms industry on electronic goods rather than artillery

What I'm worried about is the lack of military build-up that we've got in Canada—the pusillanimous approach to our own defence. Down in Newfoundland, we can hardly sleep for wondering when St. Pierre and Miquelon are going to invade.

Tory leadership candidate JOHN CROSBIE in 1983

deficit *n.* The bill for promises made during the most recent election campaign, paid in devalued Canadian funds to Swiss holders of government debt by employees of U.S. branch plants.

I go home and tell Mila, "God, if only we didn't have that $36-billion deficit!"

Prime Minister BRIAN MULRONEY in 1985, confiding that Canada's sorry fiscal affairs are intruding on his and his wife's home life

To get our financial house in order, we'll have to find a gullible mortgage broker with a wild imagination. [But] in times like these, we must remember that there have always been times like these.

Rhinoceros Party leader CHARLES MCKENZIE in 1988, setting out the party's plan to attack the deficit

delegate *v.* To pass responsibility to someone who knows what he or she is doing.

I'm busier than a whore working two beds.

Liberal cabinet minister C.D. HOWE, the most powerful member of Louis St. Laurent's government in the 1950s

I'm doing it now in the hopes that I will reach the stage like [former prime minister] Mackenzie King, *where, perhaps after many less years, I'll be able to make all the other people do the work and just go home with my diary.*

PIERRE TRUDEAU in 1969, a year after becoming prime minister

democracy *n.* The will of the people, as dictated by pollsters and implemented most effectively by elected officials of a dictatorial persuasion.

To put the multitude at the top and the few at the bottom is a radical reversion of society which every reflecting man must foresee can end only by its downfall.

SIR FRANCIS BOND HEAD, lieutenant-governor of Upper Canada, in 1839

The theory that you want the electorate to read both sides and trust to him that you are right is not practical politics.

SIR CLIFFORD SIFTON, cabinet minister in Sir Wilfrid Laurier's government

There is no greater farce than to talk of democracy. To begin with, it is a lie; it has never existed in any great country.

Quebec publisher and MP HENRI BOURASSA in 1943

Lack of absolute power corrupts absolutely.

Prime Minister PIERRE TRUDEAU during the FLQ crisis of 1970, defending the power of a strong central government to deal with civil insurrections, in a twist on Lord Acton's dictum of 1887 that "power tends to corrupt and absolute power corrupts absolutely"

The application of democracy sometimes gives me trouble. Democracy requires that you set up a lot of committees and commissions.

B.C. cabinet minister WILLIAM VANDER ZALM in 1982

It is totally antiquated. It is really a bit of a farce. Most *elections mean another dictatorship for three or four years.*

B.C. premier WILLIAM VANDER ZALM in 1986, describing the British parliamentary system

diplomacy *n.* The art of prevarication in service to a good cause.

Before I came to Paris, I thought the women of British Columbia were the most beautiful in the world. Now I think they are equal.

B.C. premier BILL BENNETT in 1977 during a trip to Paris, when asked by a reporter to comment on French women

diversion *n.* The most common magical trick: distracting the viewer's attention from the means by which the trick is performed.

The minute he won't be able to drape himself in [the constitutional] problem, we'll have him naked on the economy.

Liberal leader JEAN CHRÉTIEN in 1992 on Prime Minister Brian Mulroney's other crisis, the dismal economy

As we debate these matters, at Exhibition Stadium the Blue Jays are trouncing the Cleveland Indians 9-1 and [Dave] Stieb is pitching a one-hitter.

GREGORY SORBARA, Ontario Tory labour minister responding to a question about reforming the laws dealing with sexual assault during a legislature debate in 1988. He later apologized for the remark.

divine intervention *n.* The rarely witnessed but frequently sought assistance of an other-worldly power to solve temporal problems of an intractable nature.

An act of God.

JOE CLARK responding to a schoolchild during a classroom visit, when asked how he came to be leader of a national political party.

Clark was thirty-six years old in 1976 when he came from behind to capture the Tory leadership after finishing third on the first ballot. This didn't ensure a happy tenure in his new post, however, owing in part to the fact his victory was a stunning upset. In 1993, Tory leadership hopeful Kim Campbell, reflecting on the caucus revolts that constantly undermined Clark, said, "I wouldn't want to win the leadership on a kind of technical basis, the way Joe Clark did—not because people were saying, 'Boy, here's what we want,' but because he was the least-hated candidate in the coliseum. That might be very difficult."

It used to be the churches who asked us to wait for the hereafter for happiness, but now it is the Conservative party.

NDP leader AUDREY MCLAUGHLIN in 1992

drug test *n.* Mandatory inquiry into a political candidate's history with mood-altering substances, the use of which is deemed to qualify the aspirant as being sufficiently hip to hold office.

And I inhaled the smoke.

KIM CAMPBELL admitting in a *Le Devoir* interview during the 1993 Tory leadership race to a 1960s experiment with marijuana, playing on Bill Clinton's year-earlier confession that he had tried marijuana but had not inhaled

Those that have publicly indicated consumption of marijuana (inhaled or not) will not be refused entry to Canada (the Clinton Clause)....Many thanks and sorry for the rush but some Legislation must deal with the reckless admissions of illegal activity by aspirants (inhalants or not) to Canada's highest (no pun) Legislative and Legal Office.

letter proposing a private member's bill in Parliament in 1993 by NDP MP JAMES FULTON, who in a spirit of non-partisanship also called for a "Campbell/Charest Clause" to "ensure that those Canadians that have publicly declared consumption cannot be discriminated against." Both Campbell and leadership rival Jean Charest had admitted to marijuana use in response to reporters' questions during the leadership contest.

I was offered pot on occasion. I preferred corned beef.

Tory strategist HUGH SEGAL in April 1993, responding to reporters who wanted to know if he, like Campbell and Charest, was prepared to admit to having experimented with marijuana

Once the candidates were known, the story then shifted to such important issues as who had once smoked marijuana.

Tory leadership candidate GARTH TURNER in 1993, complaining about the media's focus on the candidates' style versus substantial issues

No. Have you got some?

Liberal leader JEAN CHRÉTIEN in 1993, responding to the obligatory do-you-ever-try-pot question

I'm not sure, in fact, that what I did brought me in breach of the law, as a matter of fact. It's not a crime to do that.

Tory leadership hopeful and former justice minister KIM CAMPBELL in Quebec City on May 22, 1993, asserting that her experiment with marijuana was not an illegal activity

I did something which I knew was illegal.

KIM CAMPBELL in Gananoque, Ontario, on May 23, 1993, backpedalling on her previous day's comment after being reminded that possession of marijuana is illegal under the Criminal Code. The former justice minister did, however, try once again to demonstrate her commanding knowledge of Canada's criminal justice system by opining that it was unlikely anyone would have laid a charge against her in connection with her marijuana use

E

economics *n.* The dismal science, of which politicians have the most dismal lack of understanding.

Q: *What does Pierre Trudeau really think about the problems of the Canadian economy when he's lying in bed at night?*

A: *When I'm lying in bed at night, I really don't think about the problems of the Canadian economy.*

Prime Minister PIERRE TRUDEAU, responding to a student's question during a televised interview

I suppose that next the government will be telling us that there is no unemployment, that it is just a nasty rumour started by a lot of people who are out of work.

Tory MP ROB PARKER in the House of Commons in 1978

Politics is marketing. Promoting British Columbia. Getting economic development. That's marketing. Running Fantasy Garden is marketing. Much in life is marketing. Even a strong marriage involves a degree of marketing....Life is marketing.

B.C. premier WILLIAM VANDER ZALM, owner of the Richmond, British Columbia, theme park Fantasy Garden, draws a parallel between politics and the role of marketing in economic development

I've learned that the trickle-down theory [of economics] is warm, wet, and amber-coloured.

an unemployed Edmonton man tells a CBC television interviewer what he thinks of Finance Minister MICHAEL WILSON's 1985 budget

election *n.* An auction where bidders buy promises, sleight unseen.

An election is like a horse race, in that you can tell more about it the next day.

Prime Minister JOHN A. MACDONALD

If you would know the depth of meanness of human nature, you have got to be a prime minister running a general election.

Prime Minister JOHN A. MACDONALD

They have just got tired of seeing us around.

former prime minister LOUIS ST. LAURENT explaining his government's defeat in 1957

What can I say? For a time this evening, I wished I were back at the University of Toronto, teaching history.

Liberal leader LESTER PEARSON in 1958, on the looming Tory landslide led by John Diefenbaker

PACR

acronym for the standard expense-account entry of 1970s-era political advance men and women who arrange election campaign events (Pissed away, can't remember)

Tonight it was our Greeks against their Greeks. On Sunday it's our drunks against their drunks.

a worker for BRIAN MULRONEY at a 1983 meeting in the Montreal riding of Saint-Denis, where agents for the rival Tory leadership candidates Mulroney and Joe Clark were vying to sign up "instant Tories" who were induced to vote for slates of delegates pledged to vote for either Mulroney or Clark at the leadership convention in June of that year. The "drunks" figured prominently in the success of Mulroney's organizers in capturing the delegate slate in the Montreal riding of Saint-Jacques, where the twenty-seven-vote margin of victory was traced to residents of the Old Brewery Mission whom Mulroney agents had bussed to the meeting with promises of free beer in return for their votes. The incident resulted in headlines, causing a Cornwall, Ontario, man to ask Mulroney during his tour of that city about the ethics of buying support with alcohol. Mulroney defended the instant voters as war veterans whose impoverished condition should not disqualify them from participation in democracy. "I didn't know you needed a $600 suit to join this party," he said.

The next election begins today.

newly elected prime minister BRIAN MULRONEY in his first meeting with his caucus in 1984

In my experience, governments are not defeated. They must grab themselves by their own lapels and hurl themselves from office.

DALTON CAMP, longtime Tory strategist, in 1985, bemoaning the inept and unsuccessful 1985 campaign by the Ontario Tory government to retain power

It would have to be the Chinese army!

New Brunswick premier RICHARD HATFIELD in 1987, on being advised by an aide not to concede defeat until the Army vote, which comes in last and can swing close seats, is counted. Hatfield's government was defeated, failing to win even one seat.

We are just concerned as their camp is that our good Rhino supporters are going to mistake the name of John N. Turner for mine on the ballot.

Rhino candidate JOHN C. TURNER in 1988, responding to Liberal concerns that their candidate in the riding of Vancouver Quadra—none other than party leader John Napier Turner—would be mistakenly overlooked in favour of the Rhino candidate bearing a similar name.

We cannot fool all of the people some of the time, or even some of the people all of the time—but if we can fool a majority of the people at election time that's all the time we need.

CHARLES MCKENZIE, leader of the Rhinoceros Party, in 1988, unveiling the party's campaign promises, which included making the month of February a national holiday, giving Newfoundlanders freedom of screech (a rum-based Newfoundland liquor), and an automatic review of party leadership every thirty minutes. The party, confident after having garnered 99,178 votes in the previous federal election in 1984, noted that among its strengths going into the 1988 election was its financial prowess: the Rhinos boasted a campaign war chest that was $6 million and 54 cents larger than that of the Liberals. "We have 54 cents in the bank," noted McKenzie, while the Liberals at that time were rumoured to be about $6 million in debt.

Of all the leadership conventions I have attended, either as delegate or media functionnaire, this Tory one now playing out in the national capital has been the most irrepressibly good-natured.... The choice of the delegates is really limited to two, both of them palpably incapable of doing any considerable damage to the country....

DALTON CAMP, columnist and former Tory party president, in 1993; the choices to which he referred were Kim Campbell and Jean Charest

empathy *n.* An appeal to voters based on the assumption that people want to be led by someone who makes a public display of commonplace foibles and inadequacies.

I have my share of heart. I have my share of mind. I am what I am.

JOHN TURNER, shortly after becoming Canada's 17th prime minister in 1984, and before launching a general election campaign in which he betrayed his Bay Street roots by referring to voters as "shareholders"

employment adjustment opportunity *n.* A job cut in the public service.

We are looking at a range of employment adjustment opportunities. The numbers are not something seen or approved by cabinet or discussed with the union.

BRIAN CHARLTON, head of Ontario's Management Board of Cabinet, in 1993, on the eve of government negotiations to pare salaries and cut jobs in the province's 950,000-strong government workforce

empowerment *n.* Screw it, *you* make the tough decisions, and *you* take the blame; an abdication of responsibility by leaders in the guise of sharing power with the followers.

Hell, you know when IBM begins to use it, it's a totally debased word.

Ontario NDP strategist DAVID REVILLE in 1991, trying to extinguish his colleagues' rapture with the buzzword "empowerment"

There's not much new there, except the bad one that allows MPs to vote from their golf carts.

Liberal leader JEAN CHRÉTIEN in 1993, commenting on parliamentary reforms suggested by Tory leadership candidate Kim Campbell, which included a proposal to allow MPs to phone in their votes from outside the House of Commons. "The more one saw of [Kim Campbell]," Mordecai Richler wrote in the June 1993 issue of *Saturday Night* magazine, "the less there was, or so it seemed. There was all that meaningless gabble about 'the politics of inclusion,' which suggested that the rest of us, like it or not, were now part of her Political Science 101 seminar. Suddenly it appeared that she wasn't running for prime minister, but, instead, wanted to be the loquacious head guide to a democracy theme park."

endorsement *n.* Fawning with damp praise.

The difference between Bill Bennett and W.A.C. Bennett is that when Bill Bennett goes to Victoria, he takes the ferry and when W.A.C. goes he walks.

B.C. entrepreneur and Bennett family friend HERE CAPOZZI on the father-and-son team of B.C. premiers W.A.C. and Bill Bennett

His re-election as prime minister will be good for Canada.

BRIAN MULRONEY in 1982, endorsing longtime rival Joe Clark shortly before entering the race to succeed him as Tory leader

Unlike some who have written [Mulroney] off, I would never underestimate a French-speaking Irish Canadian.

former U.S. president RICHARD NIXON in 1992, speaking at Conrad Black's annual Hollinger Dinner in Toronto

enemies *n.* Friends who have not yet voted against you.

If somebody's gonna stab me in the back, I wanna be there.

Toronto mayor, ALLAN LAMPORT

I have no enemies, I swear to you, I have no enemies.

Tory leader BRIAN MULRONEY in 1983

Friends, but above all, an enemy.

BRIAN MULRONEY on the two things you most need in politics

From your friends at the office....There's something wrong. There's an "s" on friend.

MICHAEL WILSON, reacting to the inscription on a birthday card he received while minister of finance

I know that there'll be fights, and I know there are going to be challenges, and I know that the enemies of Canada will not be happy.

Prime Minister BRIAN MULRONEY in 1992, kicking off his bid for a Yes vote in the referendum on the Charlottetown constitutional accord by labelling No voters as the enemy. Mulroney spent the rest of the ill-fated referendum campaign retreating from the comment.

The enemies of Canadians...are those people who are telling Canadians that debt and deficits are not a problem.

Tory leadership candidate KIM CAMPBELL during a debate with fellow candidates in 1993. Rival leadership hopeful Jean Charest offered a more generous assessment of those who disagree with the Tories' anti-deficit policy, saying, "Obviously people who don't agree with our ideas are as Canadian as we are. They have a right to disagree."

Enemy of Kim's Canada.

popular button sported by anti-Tory lobbyists within days of KIM CAMPBELL's assertion that people who disagreed with her deficit-fighting stance were enemies of Canadians

environment *n.* The most rhetorically polluted of political issues.

Those trees weren't put on that mountain by God to be praised, they were put there to be chopped down.

"FLYING PHIL" GAGLARDI, minister of public works and social improvement in the Social Credit government of W.A.C. Bennett. Gaglardi, who also served as minister of highways, earned his nickname when he was stopped for speeding in 1952 and told the patrol officer, "I wasn't driving too fast, I was flying too low."

We're getting environmental Band-Aids when we need intensive care.

B.C. NDP leader MICHAEL HARCOURT in 1989. In 1993, soon after taking office, the Harcourt government not only approved commercial logging in the old-growth forest region of Clayoquot Sound but for good measure purchased shares in MacMillan Bloedel Ltd., the company poised to harvest the trees

Let's cut down the trees and create jobs.

B.C. premier WILLIAM VANDER ZALM

I've always been interested in going to visit the people in my own province who are very hostile to the forest industry. They invariably live in nice log houses and have wood-burning fireplaces.

Tory leadership candidate KIM CAMPBELL in 1993 on the doubtful sincerity of environmentalists

evasion *n.* The art of answering difficult questions without saying anything.

For me to be able to instruct you in that would take a great deal of time.

characteristic dismissal of reporters' questions by Prime Minister JOHN DIEFENBAKER

We're not going to allow the prime minister to descend to the grubby level of discussing unemployment.

JIM DAVEY, speechwriter to Prime Minister Pierre Trudeau, responding to criticism about the lack of substance in Trudeau's speeches

Q: *What shall we do about the Abortion Bill?*

A: *Pay it!*

attributed to Prime Minister PIERRE TRUDEAU, responding to an aide

As your very busy premier, the facts are not always at my fingertips.

Quebec premier ROBERT BOURASSA ducking a question in 1974

I would suggest that the genius of the minister of finance speaks for itself.

Prime Minister PIERRE TRUDEAU in 1981, declining to rush to the defence of his embattled finance minister, Allan MacEachen

I have to be like somebody's wife. Who was it, Nero's wife or Caesar's wife? I'm like Ivory soap, purer than pure.

Justice Minister JOHN CROSBIE in 1985, reacting to new conflict-of-interest guidelines for cabinet ministers in the midst of a controversy over the appointment of Crosbie's two sons as federal legal agents

I am not denying anything I did not say.

Prime Minister BRIAN MULRONEY in 1986, saying he would submit to drug tests. A drive to submit politicians and bureaucrats to drug testing was underway in the United States at the same time.

How did you like my courageous silence on abortion?

Prime Minister BRIAN MULRONEY to an aide after a televised debate in 1988 in which he dodged the abortion issue

The smart candidate avoids detailed policy statements for they rarely help and can do you harm. Your answers should concentrate on style.

B.C. premier WILLIAM VANDER ZALM

That's agriculture.

Tory solicitor general DOUG LEWIS avoiding reporters' questions during the 1993 Tory leadership race about candidate Kim Campbell's admission that she smoked marijuana once in the 1960s

expectations, lowered *n.* The effort to appear highly accomplished, having first engineered a decline in the standard of measurement.

There are no spectacular choices in a country like Canada.

Prime Minister PIERRE TRUDEAU, campaigning for re-election in 1972

We do not have a very good track record. Our products have not been of the highest quality. Our deliveries have been lacking in reliability. Our expertise has been in large measure borrowed. Our technology has been purchased. What the hell makes us so special?

Prime Minister BRIAN MULRONEY running down his country and diminishing expectations of what he will be able to accomplish in his new job in a 1985 interview with *Fortune* magazine

explication *n.* The politician's plead: guilty with an explanation.

Canada is a hard country to govern.

characteristic remark of Prime Minister JOHN A. MACDONALD. Prime Minister Wilfrid Laurier complained, "This is a difficult country to govern," and Prime Minister Lester Pearson said, "It has been said that Canada is the most difficult country in the world to govern." Prime Minister Brian Mulroney concurred, telling reporters in his riding of Manicouagan in 1986, "This is a difficult country to govern."

I can't accept that businessmen have to rely on the post office to make a living. If they do, they'd better find other ways.

ANDRÉ OUELLET, minister responsible for Canada Post in the Trudeau government, shrugging off complaints that postal disruptions in 1981 were choking off the cash flow of small businesses

There's no question of health whatsoever. What there is is a question of aesthetics.

federal fisheries minister JOHN FRASER in 1985, shortly before quitting the cabinet after it was revealed he had overruled his own department officials and released for public sale almost one million tons of rancid tuna

[It has] good but not necessarily correct insights.

former Ontario premier WILLIAM DAVIS in 1993, praising an award-winning book, *How Petro-Canada Pumped Canadians Dry*. This account of Ottawa's treasury-draining investment in the oil patch finds a parallel with the Davis government's similarly ill-fated purchase of the oil company Suncor Inc. in 1981

You would have thought that we had engaged in a mass slaughter of the Canadian beaver.

KIM CAMPBELL in 1993, reacting to hostile media coverage of her government's decision to slash the subsidy to VIA Rail

Even politicians are human.

Prime Minister PIERRE TRUDEAU

I am human. I am a person. And I would like to be considered as such by the media and others.

Tory leadership hopeful KIM CAMPBELL during the 1993 leadership race, protesting that too much had been expected from her, and that "[she] was a bit worried about the treatment [she] received in the media as a person without weaknesses." Campbell made the observation after a torrent of said weaknesses were revealed as the leadership vote approached

external affairs *n.* A relatively safe haven among cabinet posts, since the lack of scrutiny to which foreign policy is subjected is nicely matched by the lack of interest in Canada by the nations in which it is implemented.

Foreign policy is merely domestic policy with its hat on.

LESTER PEARSON, diplomat and future prime minister

Diplomacy is letting someone else have your way.

LESTER PEARSON, external affairs minister in Louis St. Laurent's government

I'm the prime minister of Canada, I live here, and I'm about to go and have a leak.

Prime Minister LESTER PEARSON in 1967, during a meeting between Pearson and U.S. President Lyndon Johnson, whose Secret Service detail had taken over Pearson's cottage retreat. At one point, a Johnson guard asked Pearson, "Who are you and where are you going?"

We are in some ways the cheap date of NATO.

Defence Minister KIM CAMPBELL in 1993, arguing against cuts in Canada's commitment to the North Atlantic Treaty Organization and other forms of military preparedness

F

face time *n.* The imperative to raise one's profile by means of frequent media appearances, in the expectation that the substance of what was said will be forgotten but the happy, sincere face of the politician will leave an indelibly favourable impression.

Nobody can rise, unless it's against criticism. The media helped me tremendously in that, because criticism by the media is good....They have to be critical, constructively so. Even a kite can't rise with the wind, it's got to go against it.

B.C. premier W.A.C. BENNETT

Scrum of the earth.

popular 1990s expression among B.C. politicians and the reporters who cover them for the journalistic equivalent of swarming, in which a gaggle of reporters conduct a "scrum" by surrounding a politico as he or she emerges from a meeting and shoving microphones into the elected official's face

People just read the headlines. The secret of political success is getting the press—with or against is immaterial as far as I'm concerned.

Vancouver mayor TOM CAMPBELL in 1973

favourite son *n.* A political candidate propelled into a larger arena that he or she now commands by supporters who live in the same neighbourhood.

The French-Canadian people are royalist. What they want is a king.

Montreal mayor JEAN DRAPEAU justifying his autocratic tendencies while at the same time rebuffing entreaties to enter the larger forum of province-wide politics, fearing, correctly, that mayors "don't travel well." David Crombie, popular mayor of Toronto in the 1970s, learned this lesson the hard

way when he gleaned little support in his 1984 bid
for the Tory leadership

About 99 percent of the Newfoundland delegates will be supporting me...and if we can find the other fellow, he'll never make it across the Gulf.

JOHN CROSBIE in 1983 prior to the Tory leadership
convention, at which he received support from 94
percent of the province's delegates

financially challenged *n.* Broke.

The financially challenged Newfoundland government departed from Canadian political tradition yesterday by bringing down a pre-election budget without any vote-grabbing handouts. "Once upon a time it was possible to do a budget with election goodies....We didn't have that luxury," Finance Minister Winston Baker told reporters.

news report, the GLOBE AND MAIL, April 1993

free market *n.* You're on your own, pal; minimalist government, with the odd exception for a grant-seeking company or industry with pull.

When you give money to people you call it welfare. When you give money to business you call it grants. Well, I'm changing that. From now on, when we give money to people it'll be grants, and when we give money to business, that's welfare.

B.C. premier DAVE BARRETT speaking to the B.C. Federation of Labour in 1975

Government sets up the law courts and administers the arms services. It shouldn't be anything else.

Tory leadership candidate PETER POCKLINGTON in 1983, advancing his argument for minimalist government—a position that clashes violently with his own intimate government dealings. When Pocklington's Fidelity Trust collapsed in 1983, the Canada Deposit Insurance Corp. was obliged to bail out his depositors to the tune of $359 million; in 1986 the Alberta government financed his $52.5-million purchase of Palm Dairies. The Saskatchewan government was prevailed upon to bankroll in the amount of $6.2 million his plan to build a bacon plant; his Gainors meatpacking empire gobbled up $67 million in provincial loans and guarantees in 1988 before defaulting. And in 1993, a decade after his call to get government off business's back, Pocklington threatened to move the Edmonton Oilers hockey franchise to Hamilton unless the city granted him subsidies for use of Northlands Coliseum

The notion that free enterprise exists has got to be acknowledged as being a myth. If I had a choice between believing in free enterprise and Santa Claus, I'd tell you I believe in Santa Claus.

New Brunswick premier RICHARD HATFIELD in 1973

The individual least reliant on the state is the freest of all.

B.C. premier WILLIAM VANDER ZALM in 1986

I'm always available to improve the economy of Canada.

industrialist FRANK STRONACH, chairman of auto-parts maker Magna International, in 1986, two years before his failed attempt to win a Toronto-area seat for the Liberals and the subsequent near-bankruptcy of his over-leveraged firm, to which he was obliged to turn his full attention by the late 1980s

free trade *n.* A sinister plot to surrender Canada's economic sovereignty and/or furnish the thriving industry in anti-American commentary with material with which to fashion a living.

With my utmost effort, with my latest breath, will I oppose the veiled treason which attempts by sordid means and mercenary proffers to lure our people from their allegiance [to Britain].

Prime Minister JOHN A. MACDONALD in 1891, campaigning against the Liberal platform of free trade with the United States

Free trade in energy with the Americans is like wife-swapping with a bachelor.

Tory energy minister RAMON HNATYSHYN in 1979, six years before his own government embraced a Canada-U.S. free trade pact

Free trade with the United States is simplistic and naïve. It would only serve to diminish our ability to compete internationally.

Tory MP and future finance minister and free-trade promoter MICHAEL WILSON in 1983

It's terrific until the elephant twitches, and if it ever rolls over, you're a dead man.

Tory leadership candidate and future prime minister and free-trade promoter BRIAN MULRONEY in 1983

Don't talk to me about free trade....All that would happen with that kind of concept would be the boys cranking up their plants in the United States in the bad times and shutting their entire branch plants in Canada. It's bad enough as it is.

Tory Opposition leader BRIAN MULRONEY in 1983, two years before his conversion to free-trade advocacy

It is likely that the higher profile the issue attains, the lower the degree of public approval will be. The public support generated should be recognized as extremely soft and likely to evaporate rapidly if the debate is allowed to get out of control so as to erode the central focus of the message. At the same time a substantial majority of the public may be willing to leave the issue in the hands of the government and other interested groups if the government maintains communications control of the situation. Benign neglect from a majority of Canadians may be the realistic outcome of a well executed communications strategy.

a leaked government document, circa 1985, explains the necessity of keeping details about a proposed free-trade deal between Canada and the United States to an absolute minimum

fundraising *n.* The necessary first act in a political expedition, from which prevarication, betrayal of promises, and assistance to helpful friends in need can then proceed.

I must have another $10,000.

Prime Minister JOHN A. MACDONALD in a telegraphed message to CPR promoter Sir Hugh Allan, pleading for last-minute campaign funds. The publication of this document precipitated the Pacific Scandal, which cost Macdonald his bid for re-election.

It cost more when the Liberals were in power.

an unapologetic Quebec premier MAURICE DUPLESSIS, responding to the allegation of an opposition Liberal member that Quebec City tavern keepers were obliged to pay $500 annual fees to Duplessis's Union Nationale party in order to retain their licences

Love everybody, avoid the issues, and get the cheques.

Ontario premier WILLIAM DAVIS in 1975, advising Tory candidates and fundraisers on election-eve strategy

G

geography *n.* Knowledge of activity in distant precincts, a grasp of which is not mandatory for attaining elected office.

Biafra? Where's Biafra?

Prime Minister PIERRE TRUDEAU's response when asked for his reaction when Nigeria forcibly re-annexed a secessionist Biafra

This Singapore—is it in the Commonwealth?

B.C. premier WILLIAM VANDER ZALM, preparing to meet a dignitary from Singapore, which has been a member of the Commonwealth of Nations since gaining its independence from Britain in 1959

grip and grin day *n.* A day set aside each week for pressing the flesh with visiting delegations of Girl Guides and quasi-exotic local and foreign dignitaries, who arrive bearing modest, usually corny, gifts and depart with photographic mementoes of their fleeting moment of celebrity standing beside the prime minister, MP, premier, or mayor.

H

heckler *n.* A self-appointed tribune of the people whose contributions to public discourse are often prompted by over-indulgence in spirit waters—except in the case of parliamentarians in debate, whose inhibitions are notably lacking.

If you want to see me again, don't bring signs saying "Trudeau is a pig" and don't bring signs that he hustles women, because I won't talk to you. I didn't get into politics to be insulted. And don't throw wheat at me either.

Prime Minister PIERRE TRUDEAU in 1969, on a visit to Saskatoon

Mangez de la merde!

Prime Minister PIERRE TRUDEAU in 1970, shouting at striking federal mail-truck drivers. Translation: let them eat shit, a variation of Marie Antoinette's reply, when told the people had no bread, that they should eat cake.

historical revisionism *n.* Funny, that's not how I remember it, but then I'm not keen to relive the embarrassment.

Quebec has been disadvantaged in the auto industry since Confederation.

Quebec industry minister RODRIQUE TREMBLAY in 1979. The act of Confederation that created Canada in 1867 precedes the emergence of the modern auto industry by about a generation.

Gentlemen by the bar...gentlemen by the bar....There's a rule in this campaign that anyone talking except the candidate picks up the bar bill.

Tory leadership candidate BRIAN MULRONEY in 1983, interrupting an Edmonton speech to silence the chatter at the back of the room. Mulroney, who had sworn off alcohol three years earlier and forbade its use at campaign events, later denied that this one exception to his rule had occurred, telling a Global Television audience that "there has never been an open bar, there has never been a bar at any one of my meetings."

I am still, you know, looking at what the brighter side of it was and saying, "Ya, but during those times we did have order." And things were principled.

Dutch immigrant and B.C. premier WILLIAM VANDER ZALM, reflecting on the good side of the Nazi occupation of Holland

DAVID KING, Kelowna TV Host, interviewing JUDI TYABJI, Liberal candidate for the B.C. legislature, about her campaign literature in 1991:

DK: *It was brought to my attention last week, in fact, that you weren't an executive assistant to John Turner....*

JT: *It was an executive assistant to John Turner through the national revenue committee.*

DK: *It doesn't say that here, Judi.*

JT: *If it's not there it must be omitted....I worked for the national revenue committee. My position was executive assistant—that's through the office of John Turner. Bob*

Annable...was the chairman of the national revenue committee.

DK: *Either you were an executive assistant to John Turner or you worked for Bob Annable as an executive assistant.*

JT: *Would it make you feel better if it said "former executive assistant to John Turner through the national revenue committee"?*

DK: *I don't see why John Turner was mentioned at all.*

JT: *The only reason I didn't put national revenue committee is no one knows what it is.*

DK: *But, Judi, it looks better for you to say you were an executive assistant to John Turner and that's why you did it.*

JT: *It is the truth there, I just haven't included....*

DK: *What you've done is you've embellished it.*

JT: *I have not. I have edited it....It's for the sake of brevity...and every word of that is absolutely true.*

DK: *Some people are saying right now, Judi, that it's an embellishment of the truth....*

JT: *It's hardly an embellishment. It's an editing.*

DK: *It looks better to say you were an executive assistant to John Turner.*

JT: *That was my position, David. That was absolutely my position.*

[I am a] 19th century Liberal in the tradition of Edmund Burke.

Tory leadership hopeful KIM CAMPBELL in 1993, betraying a faulty grasp of Burke's record as a prominent critic of liberalism, and a prime architect of 19th-century conservatism—a movement opposed to the liberal tenets of individualism and rationalism

humility *n.* Grace before the fall.

I am here because I am not particularly obnoxious to anybody.

attributed to SIR JOHN ABBOTT, prime minister of Canada from 1891 to 1892

I'm not the greatest. I'm the best available.

Tory leader JOE CLARK in 1977

Tell me another profession where you are forgotten so quickly if the tide turns against you.

Tory MP JOHN CROSBIE in 1980

When I was honoured to lead the Conservative Party to the greatest victory in the history of Canada, I got 50 percent of the vote, which meant that at the height of my popularity, the greatest ever in Canadian history, half of the people were opposed to me that very day.

Prime Minister BRIAN MULRONEY in 1987, reflecting on his 1984 victory

Don't worry about me. I never lose an election.

Alberta premier RALPH KLEIN in 1993, on the eve of a stunning election victory in which his party recovered from a huge deficit in the polls to subdue a threat posed by the Opposition Liberals to end twenty-one years of Tory rule

humour *n.* A principal means of political self-preservation.

I never told a funny story in my life.

ARTHUR MEIGHEN, coming to grips with his slight impact in Canadian political history during his brief tenure as prime minister in 1920-21 and 1926

The worst thing about becoming premier was having to resign from my sense of humour.

ED SCHREYER, premier of Manitoba from 1969 to 1977, in 1978

hyperbole *n.* Sound and furious exaggeration, signifying nothing.

The question really, in political terms, is is being blessed by big business a little bit like being blessed by the Ku Klux Klan?

Liberal senator MICHAEL KIRBY in 1988, denouncing Tory support from the business community

[They call it a] diabolical plot to go right for the gonads of sovereignty of this country.

Trade Minister JOHN CROSBIE in 1988, defending his government's policy of free trade between Canada and the United States by attempting to discredit the critics

I can't believe the [Kim Campbell] delegates are at Jonestown. I guess they are, but I can't believe they're about to drink the Campbell Kool-Aid.

BILL MCKNIGHT, Tory energy minister and supporter of Jean Charest's bid for the party leadership, in 1993, equating Campbell's supporters with the 900 followers of cult leader Jim Jones who committed mass suicide in 1978 in Jonestown, Guyana, after drinking Kool-Aid laced with cyanide

I

ideology *n.* A set of fiercely held ideas based on high principles and defended to the death save that any fail to find favour with the voting public.

Avoid any specific discussion of public policy...at public meetings.

QUINTUS CICERO

There are dangers in spelling things out. If you propose a change, those who are threatened by it will remember it, while those who will benefit just dismiss it as another political promise.

Prime Minister JOE CLARK in 1979

The Prime Minister of Canada is no place for a philosopher. If you're going to philosophize, then you should do that in the sanctity of one of our finer universities.

Tory leader BRIAN MULRONEY, fixing the blame for Pierre Trudeau's shortcomings on his preoccupation with ideas

When I was a boy in High River I used to lie in the fields and study the heavens. And I noticed a very peculiar thing about birds. They have two wings, a left wing and a right wing. And if they had only one wing, they would fly around in circles.

characteristic story told by JOE CLARK when campaigning, warning partisans against ideological extremism

When one's left wing is not working, one tends to fly around in circles a great deal.

BOB RAE, NDP MP and future Ontario premier, in 1981

It's not the business of political parties to take hard ideological positions.

Tory leader JOE CLARK in 1983

Bill, I got a piece of advice for you. Please. Stay in the middle! Don't go too far to the right. Stay in the middle.

retiring B.C. premier BILL BENNETT in 1986, to his successor, William Vander Zalm

image *n.* The candidate's carefully nurtured public persona, widely recognizable except to the elected official's inner circle of friends and family.

[It] tells what I love most: order, beauty, the world, the universe.

AMOR DE COSMOS, British Columbia premier from 1872 to 1874, explaining why he changed his name from John Smith

So far, we've had nothing but props and music. The curtain goes up and the play never begins.

GRATTAN O'LEARY, newspaper editor and Tory senator, in 1968, on the incoming Trudeau regime

People's lives do not have to be drab and dreary and wrapped in old newspapers.

JEAN DRAPEAU, defending his flamboyant style in conducting the civic affairs of Montreal

Some commentators have suggested that I do not really exist, that I am the figment of the imagination of certain newspaper columnists and television producers. Personally, I reject this extreme view.

PIERRE TRUDEAU, a few weeks before becoming prime minister in 1968

If you meet somebody, and you're seen to be happy and smiling and pleasant, that's how people remember you, even if afterwards you're not that way.

B.C. premier WILLIAM VANDER ZALM

Style is substance.

WILLIAM VANDER ZALM, unapologetic about the lack of policy in his campaign, on the eve of winning the biggest victory of any premier in B.C. history, in 1986

Charisma without substance is a dangerous thing.

KIM CAMPBELL, candidate for the leadership of the B.C. Social Credit party in 1986, in a veiled reference to her ultimately successful rival William Vander Zalm. Campbell's own aggressively substance-shy bid for the federal Tory leadership in 1993 prompted Judy Rebick, head of the National Action Committee on the Status of Women, to crack, "Feminism without substance is a dangerous thing."

I am probably one the few people here who has not seen everything that Bill Clinton has said because I don't watch television and my view is that I believe that Canadians have to make their own politics....But my views are my own, and if President Clinton has copied them, good for him.

Tory leadership hopeful KIM CAMPBELL in 1993, responding to a British reporter's insistence that her political style is modelled on the successful campaign strategy Bill Clinton employed in the 1992 U.S. presidential campaign

inflation *n.* The debased currency with which political promises are funded.

When you spend money abroad it is not inflationary.

Prime Minister PIERRE TRUDEAU in 1968

We've got inflation licked.

PIERRE TRUDEAU in 1970. The prime minister noted that "unemployment is a regrettable side-effect of combatting inflation."

What do the Bishops know? They're not economists.

Prime Minister PIERRE TRUDEAU in 1993, responding to criticism of his government's anti-inflation policy by the Canadian Conference of Catholic Bishops

insolence *n.* Power tends towards contempt, and absolute power stokes absolute contemptuousness.

Give us twenty years and you will not recognize this country.

Tory leader BRIAN MULRONEY, speaking in the House of Commons in 1984

Don't mess with me: I've got tanks.

newly appointed defence minister KIM CAMPBELL issues a warning to the press in 1992

integrity *n.* An unwelcome hindrance to the expedient administration of the public's business.

John, I wonder if God Almighty ever made a man as honest as you look.

Prime Minister JOHN A. MACDONALD to his cabinet colleague "Honest John" Carling

invective *n.* Pleasantries exchanged among political combatants, worthy of corporal punishment if overheard in a schoolyard but deemed an essential element of parliamentary discourse.

One strong point I admire about Sir Oliver Mowat is his handwriting.

Prime Minister JOHN A. MACDONALD, finding something praiseworthy about Ontario premier and frequent adversary Oliver Mowat

Jean Lesage is the only person I know who can strut sitting down.

JOHN DIEFENBAKER on Quebec premier Lesage

Never in Canadian history has there been a government so prone to be prone.

JOHN DIEFENBAKER in 1966, critiquing the Liberal government of Lester Pearson

I will never ascribe to this government such wrongdoing as mere stupidity will explain.

JOHN DIEFENBAKER, Conservative Party leader, attacking the Liberal government in 1966

Flora MacDonald is the finest woman to have walked the streets of Kingston since Confederation.

JOHN DIEFENBAKER's putdown of longtime Tory worker and Kingston, Ontario, MP MacDonald, who was a minor player in the ouster of Dief as Conservative leader in 1967. In the aftermath of his failed 1976 bid for the Tory leadership, Brian Mulroney constantly referred to Flora MacDonald as a "fucking whore"; she had supported Joe Clark instead of Mulroney at the leadership convention.

The papers say Dalton Camp is revolting. I cannot disagree.

attributed to JOHN DIEFENBAKER, referring to the Tory strategist and ringleader of the group of Tories that succeeded in ousting Dief from the party leadership

[I am not accustomed to] vaudeville on the Hill.

Ottawa mayor CHARLOTTE WHITTON expressing disapproval of Barbra Streisand's visit with Prime Minister Pierre Trudeau

The only minister sticking with Trudeau is Billy Graham.

Tory leader ROBERT STANFIELD on the declining popularity of his Liberal counterpart Pierre Trudeau

I've got to handle my Canadian friend...that asshole Trudeau.

U.S. president RICHARD NIXON in a tape-recorded White House conversation with his aides in 1973

Le mangeur de hot dogs.

Prime Minister PIERRE TRUDEAU's putdown of Robert Bourassa in the early 1970s, when Bourassa was the youngest premier in Quebec history and deemed by Trudeau to be naïve

The Tories have been, and are, ideologically reliable. They really believe the guff they espouse....[By contrast] the Liberals are the most incorrigibly opportunistic bunch of people I ever laid eyes upon....What do the Liberals believe? God only knows.

Ontario NDP leader STEPHEN LEWIS in 1975

Deserving office of Hon. Russ Doern proposed by Mayor Stephen Juba.

sign on a portable toilet presented to Manitoba public works minister Doern in 1973 by Winnipeg mayor STEPHEN JUBA, who objected to Doern's plan for much-needed public washrooms in Memorial Park, opposite the Legislature

Mr. Clark walks hither and yon, talking in low monotones for fear that his genius might be overheard by others

JOHN DIEFENBAKER's impression of Joe Clark, a longtime worker in the Tory youth wing who had once advised Dief during the depths of his unpopularity to resign as party leader

Being attacked by Joe Clark is like being savaged by a dead sheep.

BOB RAE, member of Parliament, in 1981, on former prime minister Joe Clark

There's no miraculous way to win votes in Quebec, not even by the sonorous quality of your voice.

Tory leader JOE CLARK campaigning in 1983 to keep his top party post, in a slightly veiled reference to his chief rival, Brian Mulroney

Mr. Perfection.

BRIAN MULRONEY's standard putdown of federal NDP leader Ed Broadbent, who for a time prior to the 1988 election surpassed Mulroney in popularity in public-opinion polls

[Vancouver Quadra is] an area that has recently been besieged by tourists, one of whom is a candidate.

JOE CLARK campaigning in the 1984 general election on behalf of a Tory candidate opposing John Turner, in a downtown Vancouver riding into which Turner, then a resident of the wealthy Toronto enclave of Forest Hill, had been parachuted

I only wish I knew him before his lobotomy.

KIM CAMPBELL on longtime adversary William Vander Zalm

I sometimes feel we would be better off if we towed [Newfoundland] out to sea and sank it.

Ontario Tory MP DON BLENKARN in 1990, reacting to Newfoundland premier Clyde Wells's staunch opposition to the federal Tories' Meech Lake constitutional initiative

Please. He's a fiscal nutbar. I'm a macro-monetarist.

JOHN LONG, long-shot candidate for the Tory leadership, in 1993, on comparisons between himself and U.S. presidential candidate Ross Perot

J

jurisdiction *n.* Sorry, not my table: the chronic Canadian dilemma as to whether a given problem is a federal or provincial responsibility.

Until about two seconds ago I would have said that the weather was a provincial jurisdiction, but it clearly is a federal matter and getting more so with each passing second.

Prime Minister BRIAN MULRONEY in 1993, as the sun broke through the clouds during the Vancouver summit he hosted between U.S. president Bill Clinton and Russian president Boris Yeltsin

Kimspeak *n.* The lingua franca of Kim Campbell followers.

KIMFEST: *The charismatic Campbell electoral campaign.*

KIMFOLK: *Campbell's supporters and advisers.*

KIMSHIP: *The feeling of campaign solidarity around Campbell; the inevitable nickname for the Campbell campaign jet or bus.*

"FOR KIM AND COUNTRY": *Prime Minister Campbell's patriotic election slogan.*

KIMMY DIPPING: *Attempt by Tory MPs to draw on the popularity of their leader by featuring Campbell in their ads, making personal appearances with Campbell, etc.*

KIMLET: *Non-alcoholic cocktail that will become the campaign drink. Not to be confused with Kim-Lit—the candidate's policy position papers.*

KIMONOS *(pronounced "Kim? Oh no!s"): Gun lovers, REAL women, and other organized groups miffed at Campbell.*

KIMBECILES: *Derogatory term, used by opponents to describe the pimple-faced Tories who pack public meetings and shout "Kim, Kim, Kim!"*

KIMPERTINENCE: *An irreverent Campbell quip.*

THE KIMSY RAPPORT: *Judicious use of sexual charisma, especially between the leader and the press scrum.*

a Campbell electoral lexicon devised by senior editor CHARLES MACLI in *Report on Business Magazine*, August 1993

L

leak *n.* An untimely disclosure of secret information to the press, usually with the object of undermining a political rival rather than influencing policy.

If anybody's going to leak in this government, it's going to be me.

Prime Minister BRIAN MULRONEY in 1984, furious when a post-election meeting of top-level aides was reported in a newspaper. Mulroney dispatched an inflammatory memo, with a copy of the newspaper story attached, to all who attended the meeting—which strategy was in turn promptly reported by a television network.

Liberals *n.* Members of the Natural Governing Party.

I do not say that all Grits are horse thieves, but I feel quite sure that all horse thieves are Grits.

JOHN A. MACDONALD, referring to members of the Opposition Liberal Party

Liberalism is Socialism in a silk hat.

Tory Opposition leader GEORGE DREW

In Alberta, the only protection the Liberals had were the Game Laws.

JOHN DIEFENBAKER, characteristic remark

The Liberals are the flying saucers of politics. No one can make head nor tail of them and they never are seen twice in the same place.

Prime Minister JOHN DIEFENBAKER in 1962

The Liberals are the party of government; the Conservatives are like the mumps—you get them once in your life.

Liberal cabinet minister JACK PICKERSGILL to Tory worker and future newspaper tycoon Conrad Black in 1962, quoted by Black in his 1993 autobiography

The Liberals talk about a stable government but we don't know how bad the stable is going to smell.

NDP leader T.C. (TOMMY) DOUGLAS in 1965

You will be fine as long as you remember that the Liberal Party is a great big, heartless, headless machine.

Liberal cabinet minister PAUL HELLYER

Don't let that bastard win it, Paul....He isn't even a Liberal.

Liberal cabinet minister JUDY LAMARSH in 1968, urging fellow minister Hellyer in his failed bid to prevent Pierre Trudeau from winning the Liberal Party leadership

We are in the extreme centre, the radical middle. That is our position.

Opposition leader PIERRE TRUDEAU in 1979, speaking to the Liberal International Congress

Liberals are cocktail-party revolutionaries. They don't back up their words with action.

MICHAEL HARCOURT, former Vancouver mayor and future B.C. premier, in 1987, shortly before becoming leader of the New Democrats in British Columbia

loop, in the *adj. phrase* Privy to the decisions made by the members of the highest councils. A status eagerly coveted in good times by the nakedly ambitious office-holder in need of bragging rights, and denied by the office-holder in need of an alibi when it is revealed that members of the inner circle have messed up big time.

loose cannon *n.* A renegade, often useful in betraying illogicisms within a political party, to say nothing of his or her own thought patterns.

I never say anything provocative.

JOHN DIEFENBAKER, in obvious jest, when asked about his penchant for making controversial remarks

I am not a loose cannon. I don't say things that are inappropriate.

Tory leadership hopeful KIM CAMPBELL in 1993, brushing off a spate of ill-conceived comments, including a reference to those who don't join political parties as apathetic "SOBs," those who disagree with Tory economic policies as "enemies of Canada," her explanation that she had become an Anglican in her youth to ward off the "evil demons of the papacy," and the circulation by Reform Party members of a Campbell speech at Harvard University in 1992 in which she said Canadians voted down the Charlottetown constitutional accord because they were too "ignorant" to understand it and lacked "civic competence."

loyalty *n.* More important than being right, the ability to rally around a leader who might not be.

Anybody may support me when I am right. What I want is a man that will support me when I am wrong.

JOHN A. MACDONALD in an exchange with Tory senator A.R. Dickey, who had generously offered to "support you whenever I think you are right"

Now, gentlemen, what do you think of D'Arcy McGee? I really think you will say: Not guilty, but he must not do it again.

JOHN A. MACDONALD at a dinner in honour of his longtime political ally and fellow Father of Confederation, D'Arcy McGee, in 1865

There's a recognition that you dance with the one that brung you.

BRIAN MULRONEY in 1980, explaining his purported loyalty to party leader Joe Clark, whom he privately despised

We must henceforth live by the party's eleventh commandment, which is: "Thou shalt never speak ill of another Conservative."

BRIAN MULRONEY in his 1983 speech to delegates at the Tory leadership convention, preaching the need for party unity

I don't understand those of you who are supporting a guy who's made a career out of knocking Trudeau in the last eight years. You owe everything to Trudeau. I'll go and happily defend Trudeau and his policies, because I believe in them. When I leave politics I'll leave by the front door. Nobody will ever be in a position to say that Chrétien's a prostitute.

JEAN CHRÉTIEN in 1984, campaigning for the Liberal leadership with a shot at chief rival John Turner, who had made little effort to disguise his contempt for his old boss after quitting the Trudeau cabinet in 1975

M

media *n.* Irksome but indispensable intermediary between political actors and their audience.

You are an evil old man.

GEORGE DREW, Ontario premier and federal Tory leader, to *Toronto Star* publisher Joseph Atkinson, whose paper traditionally supported Liberal candidates and who responded, "I resent being called old."

It has been interesting to read Mr. Weasel—Westell, I beg your pardon. That was a slip of the tongue.

JOHN DIEFENBAKER in 1969, referring to the *Toronto Star*'s prominent Ottawa columnist Anthony Westell

I certainly have many sins, but I generally confess them to a priest and not to the press.

Prime Minister PIERRE TRUDEAU in 1972

I don't for a moment accept, on general principles, that a free-enterprise press is unalterably opposed to any NDP government, but if you want to get down to certain specifics I suppose I could make a bloody good argument to support the theory.

Manitoba premier ED SCHREYER in 1973

Mr. Speaker, there are two visitors in the House today, Miss Conny Lingus from Cherryvale and Mr. Jack Meoff from Falkland. Please make them feel welcome.

PATRICIA JORDAN, a B.C. legislator, unwittingly introduces to members of the assembly two fictitious individuals, whose names were slipped to her by mischievous reporters from the legislative press gallery on April Fool's Day 1976.

Joe Who?

Toronto Star headline on February 23, 1976, when Joe Clark, a dark-horse candidate, won the Tory leadership race. Clark began attacking his Liberal counterpart as "Pierre Pourquoi?"

And if I can be permitted to turn a phrase, I would say that I'm kind of sorry I won't have you to kick around any more.

PIERRE TRUDEAU at a 1979 press conference at which he announced his retirement as Liberal leader, coining a variation on Richard Nixon's 1962 post-defeat comment that the press would no longer have him to kick around any more

An editorial is just one person's opinion and that person may be a turkey.

B.C. premier WILLIAM VANDER ZALM

As Marshall McLuhan said, television is a cool medium, and the House of Commons is a hot institution. A cool medium, reporting on a hot institution, creates very bad impressions.

government House leader HARVIE ANDRE in 1992, on his government's lack of popularity

[I'm] taking a naïve approach rather than a burned-out political approach.

video jockey ERICA EHM of Toronto's MuchMusic TV network explains her preference for posing simple questions of Liberal leader Jean Chrétien on joining his 1993 media entourage

They're notoriously fickle. So I sincerely expect to be left at the altar in this particular relationship.

KIM CAMPBELL in 1993, speculating that favourable media coverage of her Tory leadership bid would fade

[It] was as much an effective rite of passage for the media as it was for me....I have a different way of expressing myself, my irony gets lost in translation....I know that's a problem, but I think people want to touch bottom with a politician....Are you going to play those old games, the "getcha, gotcha" game where

you are going to grab a word out of it that it was clearly not,...[or] are you going to allow a politician to be a person?

Tory leadership candidate KIM CAMPBELL in a 1993 interview with Hugh Winsor of the *Globe and Mail*, expressing frustration with the media for a spate of reports in which, she insisted, her controversial remarks were misinterpreted or taken out of context

Ignore the media. Say goodbye to the media.

BRIAN MULRONEY in 1993 during a state visit to Washington, D.C., when asked what advice he had for President Bill Clinton. Mulroney had come under fire for taking a lavish farewell tour of world capitals, and was asked if his Washington sojourn was a business or social engagement. "Entirely social," Mulroney bristled. "We're going dancing, tomorrow morning, seven o'clock."

I would love to have you guys write what a nice, decent, gentle, thoughtful, caring, affectionate person I am. I would love to have that. But the only two headlines I really liked? The first one said "Mulroney wins big majority," and the second one said "Mulroney re-elected with big majority." Because, you know what? All the other stuff doesn't really matter. If you are in this business and you want to be prime minister, and you don't win, you don't get to be prime minister and you cannot then demonstrate what you could do with your colleagues as prime minister."

BRIAN MULRONEY in 1993, reflecting on his tumultuous relationship with the press

[The parliamentary press gallery] became infested with knee-cappers who began to attack other journalists, saying they were in Mulroney's pockets....It became unfashionable...to say a favourable word or a reasonable word.

BRIAN MULRONEY in 1993, explaining how his once agreeable relationship with the press turned sour when he became prime minister

I feel very serene, very comfortable. I just don't read the newspapers any more.

Tory leadership candidate KIM CAMPBELL in 1993, asked if media scrutiny of her life had taken its toll

metaphorically challenged *adj.* Words fail them.

You cannot roast a wet blanket.

Prime Minister MACKENZIE KING in parliamentary debate

Let's get that in black and writing.

Winnipeg city councillor SLAW REBCHUCK a civic leader in the 1950s

Remember, there's only one taxpayer—you and me.

JOHN KUSHNER, Calgary city councillor in the 1950s and 1960s, also noted for his request to a colleague, "Don't get your dandruff up."

I deny the allegation, and I defy the allegators.

Toronto mayor ALLAN LAMPORT

It's like pushing a car uphill with a rope.

Toronto mayor ALLAN LAMPORT

It has all the earmarks of being an eyesore.

Toronto civic politician ALLAN LAMPORT on an example of bad modern architecture

The guy who runs the dog pays the piper.

Toronto mayor ALLAN LAMPORT

Did she have a Shakespearean section?

Toronto mayor ALLAN LAMPORT on Caesarean sections

Keep this up and we'll have a vicious triangle.

Toronto mayor ALLAN LAMPORT, trying to end an argument

When I'm going over the cliff, I want to be there.

Toronto mayor ALLAN LAMPORT

If you forget the complications, it's all very simple.

Toronto mayor ALLAN LAMPORT

When you're talking about me, keep your mouth shut.

Toronto mayor ALLAN LAMPORT

Let's jump off that bridge when we get to it.

Toronto mayor ALLAN LAMPORT

You can lead a dead horse to water, but you can't make him drink.

Toronto mayor ALLAN LAMPORT

It would be like sticking my head in a moose.

Toronto mayor ALLAN LAMPORT, describing what it would be like to vote for a proposed measure

Children have suffered from it, if they are born.

Toronto city councillor ALLAN LAMPORT in 1964, denouncing mayor William Dennison's proposal to build birth-control clinics in the city, which would dispense, in Lampy's words, "counterceptives"

If this thing starts to snowball, it will catch fire right across the country.

former Social Credit party leader ROBERT THOMPSON

Now the only thing that remains unresolved is the resolution of the problem.

Ontario education minister TOM WELLS in 1976

All the problems of Saskatchewan are soluble.

Saskatchewan premier ALLAN BLAKENEY in 1978

The honourable member disagrees. I can hear him shaking his head.

Prime Minister PIERRE TRUDEAU in parliamentary debate

A leopard never changes its stripes.

former B.C. Social Credit cabinet minister DON PHILLIPS

We kind of had the wool pulled out from under us.

B.C. premier WILLIAM VANDER ZALM on the B.C. Medical Association's decision to refrain from assisting in drafting a provincial abortion policy

Introducing John Buchanan to this group is like introducing a dog to a fire hydrant.

Nova Scotia premier BUCHANAN is introduced to an audience by the head of a Tory women's group in 1982

If the price of conventional [oil] is X, you have a price of X plus Y for the non-conventional oil, and the international price—you know what that is—but we have indicated we will continue to subsidize the prices...so that what you would end up with would be a mix of these prices.

MARC LALONDE, federal energy minister, explaining the government's energy policy to Parliament in 1982

The specificity of the totality.

JOE CLARK, leader of the Progressive Conservative Party, in 1983

Trying to get a commitment from our own government is like trying to walk across an ocean full of whipped cream on snowshoes.

Tory MP BOB HICKS in 1986, complaining about his own government's delay in holding a debate on capital punishment

They see politicians feathering their own nests with their face in the trough.

Ontario premier DAVID PETERSON in 1990, on the self-interest of politicians as viewed by voters

This kind of piece-meal, ad hoc, hot potato approach doesn't serve Canadians.

KIM CAMPBELL in 1993, deflecting criticism of her defence ministry's proposed $5.8-billion purchase of military helicopters

Brian Mulroney has left Canada a veritable tower of Babylon.

Liberal MP BRIAN TOBIN, resisting the mood of convention-floor adulation at the Tories' 1993 leadership convention, which kicked off with a gala tribute to Mulroney's legacy as party leader

metaphorically gifted *adj.* A memorable way with words.

It was so dry in Saskatchewan during the Depression that the trees were chasing the dogs.

JOHN DIEFENBAKER

I'm also disturbed because the doctors tell me I'm as sound as a dollar.

JOHN DIEFENBAKER in 1975, recovering from an ailment at a time when the value of the dollar was plunging

We'll cross that bridge when we fall off it.

characteristic saying of Prime Minister LESTER PEARSON

It's spelt H-N-A-T-Y-S-H-Y-N, and it looks like the first line of an eye chart.

Tory MP RAMON HNATYSHYN, future cabinet minister and governor general, spelling his surname for reporters in 1976

He looks like a lawnmower gone berserk.

JOHN CROSBIE on fellow parliamentarian Herb Gray

He looks like the driver of the getaway car.

DALTON CAMP, Tory strategist, on Liberal cabinet minister Jean Chrétien, noted for his awkward gait and crooked smile

A comparison between Madonna and me is a comparison between a strapless evening gown and a gownless evening strap.

KIM CAMPBELL in 1993, on the fallout from the famous photograph

N

national unity *n.* A bedevilling issue that admirably serves to keep elected officials from mucking about with the economy, educational reform, regional disparities, industrial competitiveness, and other lesser issues.

Well, if you still want your Rocky Mountains, keep them!

RENÉ LÉVESQUE, Quebec separatist, in 1967, to Quebec federalist politician Yves Michaud

My Centennial project is to try to love Toronto.

ROBERT STANFIELD, former Nova Scotia premier recently installed as leader of the federal Tories, on a visit to Toronto in 1967

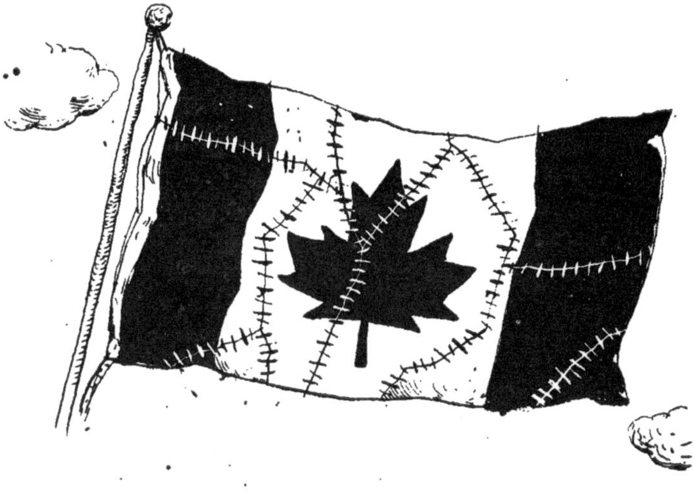

Two things hold this country together. Everybody hates Air Canada coffee, and everybody hates Ontario.

New Brunswick premier RICHARD HATFIELD

The thing that keeps this great country together is that everybody hates Ontario; and the thing that keeps Ontario together is that everybody hates Toronto; and the thing that keeps Toronto together is that everybody hates Bay Street.

Ontario premier DAVID PETERSON

That would destine it, given the dynamics of power, to eventually be governed by eunuchs.

former prime minister PIERRE TRUDEAU in 1987, on the fate of the federal government if the Meech Lake constitutional accord were ratified

I recognize that touching on the debate about Canada's constitutional future is a risky business, but then I have a hereditary defect—living dangerously.

PRINCE CHARLES in 1991, in a speech at Queen's University in Kingston, Ontario

I would like to make an appeal to reason, a call to halt the overexcited, gratuitous insults and the apocalyptic scenarios.

Parti Québécois leader JACQUES PARIZEAU in 1992, campaigning for the No side in the Charlottetown constitutional accord referendum in which his rhetoric was characterized by overexcited, gratuitous insults and flights of unreasoned fantasy

These problems have been around so long that Canada does not know how to live without them.

the London (U.K.) *Observer*'s response to the defeat of the Charlottetown accord in 1992

It's Canada's version of political gridlock, not dissimilar from the check and checkmate Americans have become used to.

USA Today's response in 1992 to the defeat of the Charlottetown constitutional accord

O

obsession *n.* Politics as an addiction, not a calling.

Men are strange about politics. I have been around the world twice and know politicians from many cultures. They are all alike. As long as they find themselves in the middle of it, they say they are sorry that all their time is taken up by politics. But as soon as they have lost and are out—oh, how terrible for them!

MARYON PEARSON, wife of Prime Minister Lester Pearson, in 1962

off the record *n.* A comment made to a member of the press in confidence, in the mistaken belief that it will stay that way.

Greed is what makes the world tick, baby.

JOHN TURNER, former federal finance minister, in a private twist on his public comment, "I doubt we can change men's motives, including the drive for material benefit."

Let's face it, there's no whore like an old whore. If I'd been in Bryce's position I'd have been right in there with my nose in the public trough like the rest of them....I hope this is all off the record. I'm taking the high road now.

BRIAN MULRONEY in 1984, campaigning for prime minister, telling reporters on his campaign plane that he could sympathize with recent patronage appointee Bryce Mackasey. Criticism of the Mackasey appointment and several other alleged patronage abuses was a main platform plank of Mulroney's campaign

official residence *n.* Taxpayer-funded lodging for a select group of top government officials, boasting above-average furnishings but alleged to serve food of a calibre only a notch above the offerings at taxpayer-funded lodgings provided for individuals who run afoul of the Criminal Code.

There are three official residences in Ottawa. There's Rideau Hall, the governor general's; there's Stornoway, where Mo and I live; and then there's 24 Sussex Drive where that other fellow is using my pool.

Tory Opposition leader JOE CLARK in 1977

Opposition *n.* A viewing gallery from which to ridicule the party in power for mistakes similar if not identical to those that the opposition can be relied upon to commit should it take power.

Being in opposition in Ontario for fifty years was not good for the [NDP]. It created unrealistic expectations. It created a sense of limitless possibilities and an addiction to rhetorical levels that simply couldn't be matched by the real world.

Ontario premier BOB RAE in 1993

Ottawa *n.* An innocuous community noteworthy for its status as the world's second-coldest national capital, warmed only by the occasional burst of overheated rhetoric emanating from Parliament Hill.

Ottawa is not a handsome city and does not appear destined to become one either.

WILFRID LAURIER

Victoria is 3,000 miles from Ottawa whereas Ottawa is 30,000 miles from Victoria.

B.C. premier EDWARD PRIOR in 1903

I long ago discovered that while it is only 2,500 miles from Vancouver to Ottawa, the distance from Ottawa to Vancouver is about 25,000 miles.

Vancouver mayor, MP and senator GERRY MCGEER

Those people in Ottawa couldn't run a peanut stand.

B.C. premier W.A.C. BENNETT on his federal counterparts in 1967

The best thing about Ottawa is the train to Montreal.

Liberal transport minister JEAN MARCHAND

panic *n.* The logical reaction to impending electoral doom, which, if not controlled, makes the grisly outcome a self-fulfilling prophecy.

There are always nervous Nellies in any organization. If they cry, they will be seen as crybabies, and the people don't vote for crybabies. They vote for people who have confidence in themselves.

Liberal leader JEAN CHRÉTIEN in 1993, trying to instill confidence in fellow Liberals panicked by the sudden popularity of prospective Tory leader Kim Campbell. Chrétien counselled his fellow Liberals not to broadcast their fears. "If you're crying and need to confess to somebody that you're nervous, don't go to the press. You come to your leader, who will tell you how to face the music."

paper trail *n.* Incriminating documents that betray unsportsmanlike conduct.

Harry, my boy, never write a letter if you can help it, and never destroy one.

Prime Minister JOHN A. MACDONALD in a letter to Col. H.R. Smith, sergeant-at-arms of the House of Commons from 1872 to 1892, referring to Macdonald's incriminating telegram pleading for a quick $10,000 in last-minute campaign funds

paranoia *n.* The well-founded suspicion that the emperor realizes the people realize the imperial wardrobe is getting skimpy.

Everyone is against me except the people.

frequent complaint of Prime Minister JOHN DIEFENBAKER

I left Holland as a kid in 1947 and I guess we got away from oppression and this is all very reminiscent of Nazi Germany.

British Columbia premier WILLIAM VANDER ZALM in 1991, equating allegations of conflict of interest directed at him with the climate of persecution in wartime Europe

Parliament *n.* The Commons and the Senate, which because of an overly attentive press suffer a reputation of being houses of ill repute.

Given a Government with a big surplus, and a big majority and a weak Opposition, you could debauch a committee of archangels.

Prime Minister JOHN A. MACDONALD in 1869

Like the devil said when he was appointed to the Senate, it's good to be home again.

T.C. (TOMMY) DOUGLAS in 1961, on accepting the leadership of the NDP

Under the present prime minister parliament has been compared to a cemetery operated by its own occupants.

JOHN DIEFENBAKER in 1970, faulting Prime Minister Pierre Trudeau for his disrespect for Parliament

I have passed around a copy of the amendments to the shareholders, the directors, er, I mean the senators.

SALTER HAYDEN, senator and director of twenty-three companies, inadvertently calling attention to the part-time nature of the job of senator, in 1975

A Senate acting as a House of Facts is essential as an antidote for the poisoning of the democratic process by professional liars.

PHILLIPE DEANE GIGANTÈS, senator, in 1990, casting veiled aspersions on his colleagues in the House of Commons

If you had to sit in that place [the legislature] year after year, as they come and go, those pre-paleolithic creatures, you would value decency and generosity.

Ontario NDP leader STEPHEN LEWIS in 1975, expressing gratitude to those few fellow MPPs, regardless of party allegiance, with an I.Q. above room temperature

party *n.* An organized collection of egos bound together less by shared ideas than by regimental discipline and a common colour scheme for the lawn signs.

Merely the struggle for office, the madness of the many for the gain of the few.

JOHN A. MACDONALD on the dubious utility of political parties

patriotism *n.* The last refuge of the obscure, attention-seeking backbencher.

Somebody who defaces the Canadian flag should be put in jail for life.

Ottawa Liberal MP MAC HARB in 1992, supporting a private member's bill sponsored by Tory MP Bob

Hicks, who insisted that "if someone thinks that little of their country [referring to anyone, according to the proposed bill, who 'burns, defaces, defiles, mutilates, tramples upon or otherwise desecrates' the flag], revoke their citizenship for two years, take their passport and tell them to get the hell out...."
The bill, inspired by a similar failed initiative promoted by U.S. president George Bush, represented an infringement of Charter of Rights guarantees of freedom of thought, belief, opinion, and expression and was defeated in the Commons.

patronage *n.* The stark realization that inferior candidates for government offices cannot be relied on to serve the public interest with the same degree of towering competence as the loyal and diligent political allies who installed you in power.

I look around this room and see a roomful of senators.

Tory leadership candidate BRIAN MULRONEY appealing to a group of patronage-hungry supporters during the leadership campaign of 1983

After I've been prime minister for 15 years and I can't find a living, breathing Tory in the country.

BRIAN MULRONEY, campaigning for the leadership of

the Conservative Party in 1983, promising party faithful that there will be plenty of patronage jobs for rival Liberals and New Democrats—eventually

You had an option, sir. You could have said, "I'm not going to do it."

BRIAN MULRONEY scores a point off John Turner in a televised debate during the 1984 general election campaign, telling Turner, then prime minster, that he should not have approved the Liberal patronage appointments that Turner inherited from the outgoing prime minister, Pierre Trudeau.

What's wrong with barbers?

Alberta premier DON GETTY in 1991, defending the appointment of his barber to the Alberta Gaming Commission

I thought it was instructive that some Conservatives, who had implored me on bended knee for appointments to the Senate and assured me of undying loyalty to the government agenda, would without so much as a by-your-leave...go the other way.

BRIAN MULRONEY in 1993, expressing outrage at the betrayal of Tory senators who helped defeat one of his government's bills in the Senate

pencil *n.* A print reporter, as opposed to the manic blow-dried geeks who file television reports. Synonym: big foot (usually in reference to a widely syndicated columnist).

policy *n.* A politician's forcefully articulated position on the crucial issues of the day, no less important than whether the politician is deemed telegenic by TV producers.

Brian tends to be pretty simplistic when it comes to strategy. He goes for the big splash. He supported Trudeau's constitutional position not because he had thought about it for five minutes, but because he was so thrilled by the sheer bravado of it all.

LOWELL MURRAY, a classmate of Brian Mulroney and Joe Clark at St. Francis Xavier College in Nova Scotia and a future constitutional adviser to none other than Mulroney in the failed 1990 Meech Lake constitutional reforms, on Mulroney's noisy support of Trudeau's effort to patriate the Canadian Constitution in the early 1980s. Within a few years of taking that position, Mulroney was vilifying that same Trudeau initiative, condemning Trudeau for having crafted a document that "left Quebec out of Confederation."

Canada is a great country and Quebec is an integral and important part of it.

BRIAN MULRONEY scribbled this platitude and several other points on a Quebecair vomit bag during the 1983 Tory leadership campaign when pressed by his aides to whip up a position statement on Quebec's role in Confederation

You're trying to wreck my holiday. Who cares about this goddam stuff?

JOHN TURNER in 1984, a few months before he would become Liberal Party Leader, on being presented with a thick summary of seventy-four key policy issues to brush up on during a getaway to Jamaica

policy reversal *n.* A post-election rite in which popular but impractical vote-getting promises are sacrificed on the altar of common sense.

Energy Minister J.J. Greene is going to publish his collected speeches—with the help of Masters and Johnson—called How to Really Enjoy Several Different Positions.

Tory leader ROBERT STANFIELD on the contradictory policy positions staked out by his Liberal adversary

Zap, you're frozen!

PIERRE TRUDEAU, campaigning against the opposition Tories' call for wage and price controls in 1974, which Trudeau then implemented in 1975

The country is broke...this country is bankrupt.

Prime Minister BRIAN MULRONEY in 1985, undermining efforts elsewhere in the government to assure depositors in a banking system shaken by the collapse of several financial institutions that a solvent Government of Canada stands ready to prevent the bankruptcy of any failing bank or trust company

The concept of universality is a sacred trust, not to be tampered with.

BRIAN MULRONEY campaigning in the general election of 1984, some years before his government introduced "clawbacks" that taxed away many government benefit payments, stripping most social programs of their universality

Only donkeys don't change their minds.

BRIAN MULRONEY in 1988, explaining his reversal on free trade with the United States

political observer *n.* A reporter's lunch buddy, usually a fellow media type whose studied observations, along with those of the cab driver who transported the reporter to a political event, are presented to readers and viewers as representative of the mood of the entire electorate. Alternatively identified as a "knowledgeable source," a "campaign insider," or a "trusted/senior/close adviser" to the politician whose actions are being reported upon by media types who must cope with unforgiving deadlines.

Press controls if necessary, but not necessarily press controls.

PIERRE TRUDEAU, prime minister and former journalist, in 1978, who despaired that media practitioners favoured insights gleaned from "political observers" over those he had picked up from frequent readings of Plato's *Republic* and flirted with the idea of imposing restrictions on media access to political events as a means of purifying the body politic

politics of pavement *n.* The maxim that some voters are more equal than others, and that their support can be bought with paved roads and other taxpayer-funded goodies.

You want roads, schools? You want your riding to make progress? Let us know about it by your votes. We will respect this expression of your desires.

Quebec premier MAURICE DUPLESSIS

I mean it when I say I am going to run a clean government.

JOHN SAVAGE, former Dartmouth mayor and leader of the Nova Scotia Liberals, in his victorious 1993 general election campaign, pledging if elected not to replace Tory government workers with Liberals after the election and to issue open tenders for government contracts, and to end the practice of awarding blacktop only to government-held ridings. Yet during the same campaign, two of Savage's own Liberal candidates insisted that all things being equal, Liberals would be hired for government posts before job seekers of dubious political affiliation. Explained one of the Liberal candidates: "Of course, you want to hire your friends, that's only common sense."

polls *n.* In recent years, the principal agent in policy formulation.

Polls are for dogs.

JOHN DIEFENBAKER, on whom the polls looked unkindly soon after his massive 1958 election victory, and ever after

All I had to do was what Martin Goldfarb told me.

Prime Minister PIERRE TRUDEAU in 1974, crediting his successful re-election to his pollster

pomp *n.* Ritualistic displays of power, more pleasing to the eye of the officeholder than public funds less obviously well spent on housing projects or daycare programs.

We don't behave like clowns, we don't behave like cornballs, we behave like a big boy, like a country which respects itself.

Prime Minister BRIAN MULRONEY in 1986, refusing to apologize for the $2.6-million cost of the "Shamrock Summit" between himself and U.S. president Ronald Reagan a year earlier

I have that done for my vanity.

Prime Minister BRIAN MULRONEY, joking with visiting journalist Michael Valpy in 1993 as the noontime gun on Parliament Hill fires

popularity *n.* The most fleeting substance in the political world.

Popularity's bad for you. I try to avoid it like the plague. And I've been reasonably successful.

Prime Minister BRIAN MULRONEY in 1992, when his popularity dipped to the lowest level ever recorded for a prime minister (in the vicinity of 8 percent)

populism *n.* A simplistic appeal to the vast majority of voters who are unimpressed by law degrees and rhetorical trickery that is made, for the most part, by office-seekers with law degrees who have mastered the art of rhetorical trickery.

I suppose [they] would find me as boring as I would find them.

KIM CAMPBELL in 1986, when seeking the leadership of B.C.'s Social Credit party. In a newspaper profile on her candidacy, Campbell described herself as a "gifted person" who enjoyed the company of intellectual equals but also likes ordinary folks "who sit in their undershirt and watch the game on Saturday, beer in hand."

That's because they know that under this cool, arrogant, intellectual, urbane exterior, there beats the heart of a Texas line dancer.

Tory leadership candidate KIM CAMPBELL in 1993, explaining her surprising support among Saskatchewan's "raunchy ranchers," as she called them

positioning *v.* The art of creating a favourable image for a product, be it an environmentally friendly detergent or a political persona.

If you eat better, you love more.

Liberal agriculture minister EUGENE WHELAN, promoting Canadian agricultural produce and his image as a populist entertainer

(1) Image is fuzzy...not certain who you are and what you stand for...

(2) it is perceived that you are not your own man—that someone else is pulling the strings—Conrad Black or some big business organization—that someone who is always perfect (changing shirts, Christian Dior shirts, Ken Doll image) should be suspicious [sic]; that you are opportunistic—here today gone tomorrow...

1983 memo to Tory leadership candidate BRIAN MULRONEY from his convention organizer John Thompson, pointing out Mulroney's perceived deficiencies

The biggest difference between selling Brian Mulroney and selling soap is that soap doesn't talk and its competitors don't say it's a crock of shit.

Tory pollster and Mulroney adviser ALLAN GREGG

You have to be a saleable commodity, someone who attracts people by your ability to do tough jobs. You also have to be interesting, different—intriguing somehow.

JEAN CHRÉTIEN in his 1985 autobiography
Straight from the Heart

posterity *n.* The cause to which politicians toil in their most ardent service.

I prefer to be chastised now and understood later.

Montreal mayor JEAN DRAPEAU

History will speak well of me because I will write it.

JOEY SMALLWOOD, Newfoundland's first premier, who spent his lengthy retirement compiling an exhaustive history of the province

post office *n.* The least-liked federal portfolio.

If we don't improve the post office, it's going to reflect badly on us. There'll be some question of our ability to run the country.

Prime Minister PIERRE TRUDEAU in 1981, instructing the new president of Canada Post Corp., Michael Warren, to make haste in improving mail service

I became defence minister instead because I don't like fighting.

PERRIN BEATTY in 1988, eagerly surrendering his old job as minister responsible for strike-ridden Canada Post Corp.

post-victory hangover *n.* One thing's for sure, the next few years won't be as much fun as the campaign.

I feel like the guy who's going through the frat house after a Saturday night party. I'm the fellow on Sunday morning who has to start pouring black coffee for everyone.

newly installed Ontario premier BOB RAE, on discovering after taking office in 1990 that the departing Liberals had not left behind an advertised budget surplus but a $2.5-billion deficit

I used to say outrageous things and nobody cared; now they hang on my every banal word.

Ontario premier BOB RAE marvelling at the transition from an Opposition leader to head of government, quoted in 1991 by Judith Timson. Rae learned the hard way the truth of U.S. president Calvin Coolidge's adage: "One of the first lessons a president has to learn is that every word he says weighs a ton."

prediction *n.* The surest means of courting political folly.

Sir John A. Macdonald is about to retire to private life, a thoroughly used-up character.

errant prediction by the *Globe*, a Liberal newspaper, in 1858, nine years before Macdonald took up his duties as the first prime minister of Canada

The Olympics can no more have a deficit than a man can have a baby.

Montreal mayor JEAN DRAPEAU, pledging that the 1976 Olympic games in Montreal would not be a drain on taxpayers. Costs rose mysteriously from a projected $310 million to $1.3 billion—an overrun for which Montrealers are still paying a special surtax.

I have it on good authority—from the roads department chief, Mr. Arpin—that it will not snow after the fifteenth of March.

Montreal mayor JEAN DRAPEAU

It's hard to make predictions, especially about the future.

Toronto mayor ALLAN LAMPORT

Prime Minister's Office (PMO) *n.* The only significant source of power and embarrassment in the federal government, its actions cloaked in the anonymity of its bureaucratic functionaries save for the one high-profile exception of the prime minister for whom they toil.

The Prime Minister's Office is the only bull that travels with its own china shop.

JODI WHITE, future manager of Jean Charest's 1993 bid for the Tory leadership, upon retiring in 1988 as

Joe Clark's chief of staff in the external affairs ministry, which was many times sabotaged by PMO directives

prolix *adj.* The abundant use of words, disguising a scarcity of thought.

I love to make him mad. You can do it by saying, innocently, that no other member has the ability to compress such small thoughts into so many words.

JOHN DIEFENBAKER in 1967, on Liberal cabinet minister Paul Martin

Ah, but don't get me started on history, because then you shall know the meaning of eternity.

JOHN DIEFENBAKER in 1971

They say I'm so longwinded it takes me fifteen minutes to clear my throat.

Ontario premier WILLIAM DAVIS in 1985

promises *n.* Solemn vows to deliver universal prosperity and happiness at an undetermined future date or, failing that, at least not to screw up as badly as the previous crowd.

The task of the politician is to climb the tree and shake down the acorns to the pigs below.

Prime Minister JOHN A. MACDONALD

He was the only man I ever knew who could get money from the rich and votes from the poor with the promise to protect them from each other.

socialist leader T.C. (TOMMY) DOUGLAS on B.C.'s Social Credit premier W.A.C. Bennett

The young people of today are going to strengthen the nation at the cost of partisan politics, and they are going to take a much more idealistic view of things twenty years from now than we do today.

BRIAN MULRONEY, age twenty-one in 1961 and executive vice-president of the Conservative Students' Federation, responding in a *Maclean's* roundtable discussion to Peter C. Newman's question, "Do you think the politician of the future will...change? What will his attitude be towards patronage, for instance?" Contemplating the concept of Senate reform with additional seats in the upper chamber many years later, Mulroney was gleeful at the prospect "of more seats than even I can fill."

When potash prices were bringing in $300-million windfall dollars a year, what happened to all the money? Where did it all go? Well, it went into buying farms and mines and all this, and we still don't have anything. When times are good, you've got to make use of it.

Tory premier GRANT DEVINE, assailing the economic record of the NDP government he toppled in 1982, which left behind a $139.3-million budget surplus. By the time Devine was defeated in 1992, the Saskatchewan government had accumulated a deficit of several billion dollars

[A] new era of national reconciliation.

one of several proposed new approaches to governance offered in the Mulroney administration's first throne speech, in 1984, which also called for "a renewed national consensus," "co-operation of all partners in Confederation," and "building a national economic consensus."

[The adjustment programs will be] among the most generous brought forward anywhere.

BRIAN MULRONEY campaigning for re-election in 1988, promising that any job loss caused by his proposed Canada-United States free trade deal would be offset by an extensive retraining program.

Following the Tories' re-election, the adjustment programs were shelved indefinitely.

In terms of total numbers, no.

KIM CAMPBELL in 1993, when asked if she could estimate the economic impact of her promise to increase a GST rebate on new homes

public opinion *n.* The most unforgiving jury. "The pressure of public opinion is like the pressure of the atmosphere," noted American scholar and critic James Russell Lowell. "You can't see it—but, all the same it is sixteen pounds to the square inch."

There is no gratitude to be expected from the public. I have found that out years ago.

JOHN A. MACDONALD

Do you wish to know what public opinion is? It is the opinion of those who are against us.

Quebec premier MAURICE DUPLESSIS

There is a certain loneliness that comes from being the leader and being the prime minister.

Prime Minister BRIAN MULRONEY in 1992

purge *n.* The periodic dismissal from one's camp of colleagues whose loyalty or efficacy is in doubt.

If I found in my own ranks that a certain number of guys wanted to cut my throat I'd make sure I cut their throats first.

Prime Minister PIERRE TRUDEAU

Q

qualifications *n.* The skill set of the successful politician, which can vary markedly from one candidate, party, and campaign to the next—although good grooming is always a must.

To the young members [of Parliament] who have just come I would say that for the first six months after you are here you will wonder how you got here. Then after that you will wonder how the rest of the members ever got here.

JOHN DIEFENBAKER's advice to neophyte parliamentarians

I didn't know the difference between the Pan-American Games and Pan American Airlines.

Winnipeg mayor STEPHEN JUBA, who climbed a steep learning curve in the course of successfully lobbying to have the high-profile Pan-Am games held in his city in 1967

SHEEP AND SWINE
Candidate City

two signs affixed to an aging pavilion behind the Ottawa Colesium, site of the 1984 Liberal leadership convention. The building served as a gathering point for informal mingling between candidates and delegates.

The long and the short of it is that we are scrambling like crazy. We are all blown away by how little any of us knows about the workings of government.

GERRY CAPLAN, longtime NDP activist, on the difficulties of his task in assisting the party in its transition from opposition to government after Bob Rae's surprise victory in the 1990 Ontario election

There is now an understanding in people's minds that the two issues are related and you do have to walk and chew gum at the same time.

HUGH SEGAL, Prime Minister Brian Mulroney's new chief of staff, in 1992 on the link between the constitutional debate and the economy

Would politics be the only occupation where experience isn't an asset?

Liberal leader JEAN CHRÉTIEN in 1993, wearying of frequent observations that at age fifty-nine and having served in several cabinet posts, he was a "yesterday's man" who compares unfavourably to bright lights such as Kim Campbell, forty-five, and Jean Charest, thirty-four. In *Familiar Studies of Men and Books*, Robert Louis Stevenson observed that "politics is perhaps the only profession for which no preparation is thought necessary."

Any columnist who wants to become a politician is like a jockey who wants to become a horse.

columnist ALLAN FOTHERINGHAM on the 1993 Tory leadership bid of MP and former business columnist Garth Turner

R

racism *n.* The low road to victory.

The sound policy and the best policy for the Japanese Canadians themselves is to distribute their numbers as widely as possible throughout the country where they will not create feelings of racial hostility.

Prime Minister MACKENZIE KING in 1944

The French, you see, have too much.

JOHN DIEFENBAKER, explaining to erstwhile adviser

Dalton Camp why it was wrong to abandon the
British Ensign for the new Maple Leaf flag, which
he mistakenly thought was designed for Quebec

He needed a distraction, a political fog, and out of the east came the sound of a frog.

B.C. premier WILLIAM VANDER ZALM skilfully crafts
a racial slur in the form of a poem
about Pierre Trudeau

That's not to say that there aren't some bad ones.

B.C. premier WILLIAM VANDER ZALM on immigrants from the Orient, who otherwise are a pretty good lot. "I have to tell you I fell in love with our Chinese community—I think they're just the most wonderful people—and as I fell in love with the Chinese, I began to realize that perhaps, though they looked alike, there was another wonderful group—the Koreans, and the Vietnamese, and they were super, as well as the Filipinos. Just [a] fantastic lot of people."

realpolitik *n.* An absence of illusions about the wiles of getting and using power.

Never retreat, never explain, never apologize. Get the thing done and let them howl.

Nellie McClung, member of the Alberta legislature from 1921 to 1926

Politics is the skilled use of blunt objects.

former prime minister Lester Pearson

Niccolo Machiavelli, you know, got a bum rap.

Liberal strategist Jim Coutts in 1984

reason *n.* A high road to victory, seldom travelled.

Nine-tenths of politics appeals to emotions rather than to reason.

Prime Minister Pierre Trudeau in 1972, reflecting on the painful experience of coming close to being thrown out of office

recession *n.* The cyclical phenomenon in which economic vitality and government popularity decline in perfect tandem.

New economic order.

Prime Minister PIERRE TRUDEAU's phrase in 1981 to describe the oncoming recession

A recession is when your neighbour loses his job. A depression is when you lose your job. Economic recovery is when Pierre Trudeau loses his job.

BRIAN MULRONEY speaking at a Tory fundraiser in 1982

We predicted a year ago that we would go into a slowdown period.... Sustainable growth can't go on forever.

Tory revenue minister OTTO JELINEK in 1990, refusing to use the word recession to describe the slide in the economy

recruitment *n.* The search for bright, young faces to peddle tired, old ideas.

I say to you let's hug them, let's kiss them, let's do anything we have to do to get them back in our camp—that's where they belong.

deputy prime minister DON MAZANKOWSKI in 1993, predicting that Reform Party members can be wooed back into the Tory camp

red meat *n.* Damaging information about the secret life of a politician, helpfully offered to the press by the politician's adversaries in a usually successful effort to distract attention from the inadequacies of their own client. Should such data be non-existent or difficult to manufacture, dissemination of the fact the targeted victim utterly lacks a secret life can be exploited as proof of unsuitability for office for lack of charisma.

A supporter told me people have been out digging for dirt on my life and all they've found is a few dustballs under my bed.

Tory leadership candidate KIM CAMPBELL in 1993

We have had dissections of [Campbell's] early life, her childhood traumas, her peripatetic career, her intellectual history, her first marriage, and even her parents' marriage....It is also fascinating to see how the biographers have reworked an old political myth to fit current obsessions: Leaders no longer build their character by overcoming early material adversity, but by overcoming early emotional adversity. Absent or bad parents are what log cabins used to be.

MARGARET WENTE, editor of the *Globe and Mail*'s *Report on Business*, in 1993, on Kim Campbell's ascension to the Tory leadership

There is no truth to the rumour that [cabinet minister Perrin] Beatty withdrew [from the Tory leadership race] because he knew that when it came to show and tell he would have been unable to confess that he had ever smoked pot, driven drunk, or even switched on the adult movie on a hotel TV channel.

MORDECAI RICHLER writing in the June 1993 issue of *Saturday Night* magazine

red menace *n.* Things would be so much worse if the commies were in power—oh look, here they come!

If you elect those CCF people, they'll take away your home, they'll take away your car, and burn down your churches. Furthermore, they'll nationalize your women.

a B.C. Liberal candidate for Parliament campaigning in the B.C. Interior in the 1930s, warning against the spectre of the socialist Co-operative Commonwealth Federation, precursor to the New Democratic Party

The insidious, vile, poisonous encroachment of communism.

GEORGE DREW, Tory premier of Ontario, greeting with dismay the 1948 election results that propelled the CCF—communists, in Drew's eyes—to the status of official opposition, an election in which Drew lost his own Toronto seat in the Legislature

The socialist hordes are at the gates.... Socialist barbarians are coming in through the back door.

B.C. premier W.A.C. BENNETT in his failed 1972 campaign against NDP leader Dave Barrett, who greeted the victorious dawn saying, "I am the socialist hordes."

If elected mayor, I would want a free-enterprise council with me, but if somehow a couple of commies came in, I'll work with them.

Vancouver mayoralty candidate WILLIAM VANDER ZALM, who failed in his bid to unseat incumbent Michael Harcourt

The only difference between a Communist and a Socialist is that they are both bears but one has its claws retracted.

former Tory premier STERLING LYON of Manitoba

The first thing Ed Broadbent would do if elected prime minister would be to nationalize Harry Rosen.

BRIAN MULRONEY in 1986. Mulroney's bewildering attack on the NDP leader was intended to remind voters either of the NDP's longstanding pledge to nationalize banks or of the ill-fitting brown tweed jackets Broadbent favoured when he first ascended to his party's leadership in the 1970s.

Any Ontario business seeking to escape the Socialist Agenda of their newly elected provincial government will be welcomed to the Portage la Prairie and Interlake area of Manitoba. For further information of this exciting offer, contact Felix Holtmann, MP, Portage-Interlake.

advertisement placed in the *Globe and Mail* by Tory MP HOLTMANN after Bob Rae's New Democrats came to power in Ontario in 1990

regional economic development *n.* The practice of buying votes in distressed regions of the country.

If you're going to have a massive, embarrassing political failure, it should be something innovative. Besides, it got me on the "Today Show." I was almost interviewed by Barbara Walters.

New Brunswick premier RICHARD HATFIELD in 1980, on the spectacular failure of his province's investment in the ill-fated Bricklin sports car.

regionalism *n.* The pattern of geographic alienations that binds the country together; no region is without another region to envy or view with contempt.

I would be quite willing, personally, to leave that whole [Hudson's Bay Co.] country a wilderness for the next half century, but I fear if Englishmen do not go there, Yankees will.

JOHN A. MACDONALD in 1865. At the time, the HBC territory took in most of what is now Western Canada.

Canada is like an old cow. The West feeds it. Ontario and Quebec milk it. And you can well imagine what it's doing in the Maritimes.

T.C. (TOMMY) DOUGLAS, socialist leader and former Saskatchewan premier

In the Conservative view, you have ten premiers and the prime minister as a kind of head waiter to take their orders.

PIERRE TRUDEAU, faulting the conciliatory line of his successor as prime minister, Joe Clark, towards the premiers, in 1979

Canada is seen by some as a confederation of shopping centres.

Prime Minister PIERRE TRUDEAU in 1981, criticizing premiers eager to grab more power for their provinces

Quebec is not a province like the others, as all children learn before playing Atari or Nintendo.

Parti Québécois leader JACQUES PARIZEAU in 1990

No one can deny that Quebec is, culturally and sociologically, a distinct society. So is Newfoundland.

EUGENE FORSEY, constitutional expert and former senator, in 1990

resolve *n.* To be fixed as the North Star, until moved by an alteration in voting preferences.

I know you shouldn't say that, but that is my decision. I can't conceive of any circumstances that would change my mind.

BRIAN MULRONEY in a 1978 interview with the *Financial Post Magazine*, still nursing his wounds from his failed 1976 Tory leadership bid, and forswearing a return to politics

rhetoric *n.* Wordplay passing for wisdom.

Fool-osophy.

dismissive term for "philosophy" coined by Alberta premier WILLIAM ABERHART as a device for reinforcing his populist appeal

To conceal thought he uses words. Indeed, as I listened to him from time to time I am reminded of someone in the United States Senate who described the tongue of a certain senator being like a race horse: the less load it carries the faster it goes.

JOHN DIEFENBAKER

Egg-cetera, egg-cetera, egg-cetera.

typical means of wrapping up an answer by Liberal agriculture minister EUGENE WHELAN

If after my talk you are still confused, as you may well be, I dare to hope that it is at least confusion on a higher plane.

diplomat and future prime minister LESTER PEARSON in a 1956 speech

Now we'll be able to figure out who's louder—Axl Rose or Garth Turner.

Ottawa city councillor JIM WATSON in 1993, on the city's decision to change its noise bylaw to midnight from 11 p.m. during the Tory leadership convention, despite protests from residents nearby the convention site. Ontario MP Garth Turner was a candidate in the race; Axl Rose is a singer with the rock group Guns N' Roses, which obtained a similar exemption during a 1992 Ottawa concert.

riposte *n.* Return fire.

Madam, I cannot conceive.

JOHN A. MACDONALD, when asked by an angry suffragette, "What is the difference between the prime minister and myself?" Macdonald was, in fact, an early advocate of female suffrage.

Madam, if I were the Angel Gabriel you wouldn't be in this constituency.

GERRY MCGEER, Depression-era mayor of Vancouver, responding to a heckler's cry, "I wouldn't vote for you if you were the Angel Gabriel."

I've never laid an egg either, but I know more about omelettes than most hens.

T.C. (TOMMY) DOUGLAS, dismissing a government member's assertion that Douglas was ill-equipped to criticize government agriculture policy because he wasn't a farmer

I am now at my full height, which is not very imposing (it is five feet six inches). Fortunately, these are houses of debate where the measurement is from the shoulders up, rather than from the shoulders down.

neophyte MP T.C. (TOMMY) DOUGLAS in 1962, responding to a heckling MP who shouted at him to stand up

Q: *If I smelt your flower would you blush?*

A: *If I pulled your chain would you flush?*

exchange between the LORD MAYOR OF LONDON and Ottawa mayor CHARLOTTE WHITTON during the former's visit to Canada's capital, who was commenting on a corsage the mayor was wearing on a low-necked formal dress

For us the greatest impact of French-Canadian culture has been made by Maurice Richard and Lili St. Cyr.

NDP MP DOUG FISHER in 1961 at a Quebec City symposium organized by Brian Mulroney and other Laval University students, in response to René Lévesque's assertion that "you [meaning English Canada] need us more than we need you." Maurice Richard was a hockey legend with the Montreal Canadiens and St. Cyr, a stripper.

The premier called me a Waffle. Well, I called him a pancake. Then he called me a double Waffle. I called him a stack of pancakes. Knowing the way he feels about Quebec, I warned him if he calls me a Waffle again, I'll call him a crêpe suzette.

B.C. NDP leader and future premier DAVE BARRETT recalling a 1972 conversation with Social Credit premier W.A.C. Bennett. The "Waffle" group was a short-lived movement of left-wing economic nationalists within the NDP and was purged from the party in the early 1970s.

Where does he think his funds come from—the United Appeal?

Ontario premier WILLIAM DAVIS in 1973, responding to accusations by the Liberal Opposition leader that the Davis government was granting favours in exchange for donations. The United Appeal was the precursor to the United Way.

Ça s'en vient, Monique. En parlant d'accouchement, Monique, ça s'en vient? [It's coming, Monique. Speaking of childbirth, Monique, is it on the way?]

BRIAN MULRONEY during his second day in the House of Commons in 1983, responding to Liberal health minister Monique Bégin, who had heckled him with the word "accouchez!"—meaning literally "give birth" but more commonly an idiom for "get to the point." Displaying bad taste and ignorance of parliamentary protocol, Mulroney seized on a response that called attention to the health minister's ample girth and had spoken to her directly by name rather than addressing the Speaker and referring to Bégin as the Honourable Minister of Health and Welfare, as Commons rules require. Tory house leader Erik Nielsen apologized to the Commons on Mulroney's behalf three days later, by which time Mulroney had arranged to alter the official Hansard version of his comment to, "I can assure the Hon. Minister of National Health and Welfare that I will get there in due time."

If you turn on a light, you're going to attract bugs.

PRESTON MANNING, leader of the Reform Party, responding to criticism of his ideas

I've now found out I'm not going to be sleeping a lot as prime minister. But that's okay, I'm young.

Tory leadership candidate JEAN CHAREST, deflecting criticism that at thirty-four he's too young to be prime minister, in a response to leadership rival Garth Turner's proposal for a toll-free 800 number

enabling Canadians to talk directly to the principal
resident of 24 Sussex Drive

Where do they think that the roast beef they had in the Parliamentary restaurant yesterday comes from?

Prime Minister BRIAN MULRONEY in 1993, responding to criticism from Opposition MPs Lloyd Axworthy and Svend Robinson, who complained about his hunting exploits after the release of a photograph of Mulroney and Russian president Boris Yeltsin posing arm-in-arm over a couple of dead boar, complete with rifles resting on their carcasses. Mulroney said that in retirement he would miss the kind of excitement this type of incident stirred up, "but not as much as the boar."

You've got the wrong guy. You want Trudeau.

Tory leadership hopeful KIM CAMPBELL in 1993, responding to a young man in an Ottawa pub who gave her a middle-finger salute

He's never really recovered since he was turned down for the lead role in Jurassic Park.

Ontario premier BOB RAE on Tory Opposition leader Mike Harris, in 1993

S

scare mongering *v.* You think we're bad, consider the alternative.

The light of democracy goes out in Ontario.

Ontario Liberal leader HARRY NIXON in 1943, predicting the consequences should the CCF come to power

second coming *n.* A politician's announced resemblance to the Saviour.

My name is Jean Chrétien, you know, it's Christian in English....My initials are "J.C." like Jesus Christ....At thirty I was at the beginning of my public life; I hope that I will not be crucified—I'm thirty-three.

backbencher MP JEAN CHRÉTIEN in 1967, on the CBC-TV show "Twenty Million Questions"

Only in politics do resurrections occur.

ROBERT BOURASSA, deposed as Quebec premier in 1976, presciently musing in 1982 about the possibility of the stunning electoral comeback he would make in being restored to the premier's post in 1985

I've been in and I've been out, I have even been buried ten feet deep. That's where Joey Smallwood said he had put me, but, like another famous J.C., I rose again.

JOHN CROSBIE in 1983 campaigning for the federal Tory leadership. Crosbie, then a Liberal, along with cabinet colleague Clyde Wells, broke with their leader, Smallwood, in disputing the efficacy of Smallwood's regional development schemes

Even I, an old optimist, will acknowledge that this comeback is going to do honour to Lazarus, believe me.

Prime Minister BRIAN MULRONEY in 1992, on the prospects for improving his party's fortunes prior to the next election. Despite hinting widely that he was game for the challenge, Mulroney announced his planned departure from the leadership post in early 1993—but only after issuing many strong assertions that he could have pulled off a third straight election victory.

self-deprecation *n.* Penance wilfully accepted as a penalty for minor shortcomings, inviting sympathy and obscuring a continued inability to address major shortcomings.

I am more than pleased to be your host this evening, Your Royal Highness, as I was the guest of your family for four years until recently.

Montreal mayor CAMILLIEN HOUDE welcoming Princess Elizabeth and the Duke of Edinburgh to Montreal in 1952, referring to the time during the Second World War that he spent imprisoned for having encouraged Quebeckers to avoid military service

The way I make a speech, people know I'm not out to impress them, so I must be telling the truth.

Tory leader ROBERT STANFIELD in 1968

Maurice Chevalier and I worked hard to keep our French accents.

Liberal MP JEAN CHRÉTIEN confronts the issue of his broken English

I have often thought that my whole political life—my whole life, as a matter of fact—could be summed up in the words "printer, preacher, politician, premier—or the descent of man."

T.C. (TOMMY) DOUGLAS, former NDP leader, in 1975

[Our son] Nicholas got lost in our shoe closet and it took us an hour to find him.

Prime Minister BRIAN MULRONEY at a Parliamentary Press Gallery dinner at the height of "Guccigate," when it was revealed that Mulroney and his wife had borrowed $300,000 in Progressive Conservative party funds to renovate the prime minister's official residence, using some of the money to build closets large enough to hold some fifty pairs of Gucci shoes

You can always pick me out of the crowd at dinner because I never fail to wear a bib.

B.C. premier WILLIAM VANDER ZALM

The latest poll shows 60 percent of Canadians think the Liberals will win the next election. The other 40 percent are Liberals.

Liberal leader JOHN TURNER in 1988

Perfection is not likely to be something associated with me.

Prime Minister BRIAN MULRONEY in 1993, reflecting on his career in a BBC interview in London with David Frost

self-exile *n.* Flight from the scene of the grime.

Which one of those idiots would you hire?

JOHN TURNER, former Trudeau cabinet minister, describing his low estimation of his former cabinet colleagues to a Montreal industrialist

separatism *n.* The urge to discuss the concept of entertaining the idea of entering into negotiations to contemplate the prospect of the implications and benefits arising from and the genuine desire of Quebeckers to think about embracing the notion of a quasi-sovereign and in many respects autonomous Quebec wholly separate from, but then again possibly linked by economic and political structures—of a very loose nature, of course—with respect to Quebec's relationship to the rest of Canada. The longest-running dramatic entertainment on the continent, even surpassing the Broadway run of Agatha Christie's equally tiresome *The Mousetrap.*

Voice in the crowd: Vive la France!

Trudeau: Si vous voulez. Vive la France, et vive les Anglais, aussi. Et vive la république des patates frites.

[Long live the French! Trudeau's response: If you like. Long live the French, and long live the English, as well. And long

live the French fries republic.]

Prime Minister PIERRE TRUDEAU campaigning in the Canadian general election in 1968.

By God, I'll boot the rear of anyone who can't speak English.

Parti Québécois leader JACQUES PARIZEAU in a 1992 *Time* magazine interview, employing one of the curious, affected Britishisms that characterize his speeches in insisting on English fluency among Quebec francophones while at the same time defending Quebec's French Language Charter, which places strict limitations on the use of English and has transformed Quebec into the most rigidly unilinguist regime in Canada

In the context of an independent Quebec, France would play a remarkably important role.

Parti Québécois leader JACQUES PARIZEAU in Paris in 1991, pitching the merits of an independent Quebec. Despite his appeals to a common heritage between Quebec and France, some members of the French National Assembly were at pains to allow that Parizeau overstated support in France for a sovereign Quebec and could not understand, as one French legislator put it, any decision by Quebec to "proclaim the independence of a micropower on the North American continent."

Quebec has put on its coat in preparation to leave, but its boots are still in the closet.

LYSIANE GAGNON, columnist for Montreal's *La Presse*, in 1991, on the degree of support in Quebec for separation

setback *n.* An untimely misfortune, offering an opportunity to appear superhuman by bouncing back. The political veteran, in contrast, say, to the decisive tycoon who flirts with taking up politics as a second career, understands that the political process is an unending series of setbacks and comebacks that more or less even out in the end, with little tangible evidence of progress having been achieved.

What else can happen to this goddam government?

Prime Minister ROBERT BORDEN, already sapped by the burdens of a conscription crisis and trying to run a coalition government, watches as the Parliament Buildings are destroyed in a 1916 fire

If I win, I win. And if I lose, I spare myself untold agony.

a philosophical JOHN CROSBIE campaigning, unsuccessfully, for the Tory leadership in 1983

I've inherited a bag of shit!

JOHN TURNER, freshly installed as Liberal leader and prime minister in 1984, on learning that the national deficit was about to hit $35 billion, the debt was rapidly climbing towards $200 billion, the jobless rate was soaring beyond 11 percent, and predecessor Pierre Trudeau had left behind a clutch of controversial patronage appointments for Turner to announce

Well, we goofed—what can I say? But I'll tell you this, I have regrouped. I love it, I have regrouped.

JACK LAYTON, purported leader of reform councillors at Toronto City Hall, after a failed effort to rally unreliable allies behind a string of initiatives

sex *n.* A subject politicians infrequently toy with only as a reminder that it is properly the field of social scientists.

The only remedies are immigration and copulation and these will work wonders.

JOHN A. MACDONALD on the keys to developing the economy of an underpopulated Canada

Mr. Speaker, won't you please bang that thing of yours on the table?

an exasperated AGNES KRIPPS, Social Credit member in the B.C. legislature, calls for silence while trying to explain her proposal to discourage the use of the word sex in everyday conversation in favour of BOLT—Biology of Living for Today. The proferred term was greeted with mockery by fellow members, who shouted, "I'm bolt upright just listening to you" and "It's okay for the bolts but what about the nuts?"

How would you like to see the member's member?

Tory MP HEWARD GRAFFTEY, frequent comment to visitors at his Ottawa residence upon alighting from the shower, as quoted by Conrad Black in his 1993 autobiography

Q: *Will you give up your Mercedes?*

A: *Are you talking of the car now, or the girl?*

Q: *The car.*

A: *I won't give up either.*

exchange between PIERRE TRUDEAU and an interviewer when Trudeau was campaigning in 1968

I can't give you too many kisses. The press is watching. Perhaps later.

PIERRE TRUDEAU campaigning in 1968, to a Liberal party worker

An exciting party should have both blondes and brunettes.

PIERRE TRUDEAU in 1968, the year he became prime minister. By "party," Trudeau left unclear whether he was referring to festive gatherings or political organizations

You know, if you eat too much beef you become ferocious and sexy.

Liberal Agriculture Minister EUGENE WHELAN speaking at a cattleman's meeting in Alberta in 1976

The time is past when people refer to love-making as "working for the sake of the country."

former federal cabinet minister GÉRARD PELLETIER in 1988, referring to Quebec's high birth rate during most of the 20th century, a practice encouraged by the church to maintain a francophone majority in Quebec. By the 1980s, Quebec's birth rate had plummeted to one of the lowest in the industrialized world.

I think there is probably a baby picture around that reveals more of me than you've seen up until now, but that's about all.

Defence Minister KIM CAMPBELL in 1993, assuring reporters in London, England, that the famous picture of her with bare shoulders was a one-shot deal

I have a tacky old housecoat on, not an evening gown.

KIM CAMPBELL in 1993, responding to reporters in London, England, who wanted to know what she was wearing behind the legal robes she held in front of her bare shoulders in the famous photograph.

"What's interesting to me," Campbell said, trying to steer the questioning to non-sexist territory, "is how many women look at that picture and see it as representing the female reality behind the role."

sexual orientation *n.* A factor sometimes held to have a bearing on competence—curiously enough, only after it has becomes a matter of public record.

The easier we make it for people to be homosexual the more we will have.

Tory MP ROBERT COATES, opposing 1968 amendments to the Criminal Code

Wouldn't that be something, Svend as minister of defence? I'll tell ya, that would make one fine ministerial meeting.

Prime Minister BRIAN MULRONEY in 1988, asking a partisan audience in Saanich, British Columbia, to imagine NDP MP Svend Robinson, who represents the nearby riding of Burnaby-Kingsway, as chief of Canada's military forces. Mulroney got the intended raucous response with his snipe at Robinson, who had recently become the first Canadian parliamentarian to make public his homosexuality.

You're running against a publicly declared homosexual....If Svend [Robinson] can say it, I can certainly say it. Now then, is that really what you want as a role model for your children?

Tory MP CHARLES COOK of British Columbia in 1988, campaigning on behalf of a Tory candidate seeking (unsuccessfully) to replace Robinson in the Commons

Thank God I've got grandchildren or I'd be called a lesbian.

NDP leader AUDREY MCLAUGHLIN in 1993, on suspicions aroused by her status as a single woman in politics

skirt *n.* A female politician who enjoys the distinction of never failing to be favoured with questions about her views on hairstyles, culinary trends, child-rearing techniques, and the noble role that men have played in her life, while attempting to outline her proposed remedies to the deficit crisis and strife in war-torn Somalia.

If women had their say in politics today, the country would be ruled by emotion rather than reason.

federal MP WILLIAM F. MACLEAN in 1895, arguing against women's suffrage

To allow women to vote is, without any necessity, to impose on them a new obligation, a new duty, in addition to those which they have already as daughters, wives, and mothers. I have too much regard for women—and this is my way to show them my respect—to impose on them a new function, to overburden their shoulders, which could not bear such a heavy burden.

parliamentarian SÉVERIN LACHAPELLE in 1895,
arguing against women's suffrage

We all admit that women are the most beautiful part of humanity. They are, so to say, the point of connection between earth and Heaven. They soothe and alleviate social evils. She is made for the house, for the home of which she is an angel. There would be much imprudence to make a voter of her, to entangle her in the acts of violence which accompany our political contests. Let us leave them their moral purity, their bashfulness, their sweetness, which give them in our minds so much charm. Providence intended that it be so.

parliamentarian GUILLAUME AMYOT in 1895,
arguing against women's suffrage

It will take away from the real charm and womanliness of women if they were given the franchise and allowed to mix in politics. I can imagine that I might go home some evening and find, instead of being expected, with tea on the table, nothing was done, because the absorbing question of the hour was politics. I might find a very nice-looking politician sitting in the parlour soliciting a vote. I am afraid that a good many married men might get tired of the situation....If the franchise were given to women, the question would not stop there. The next thing would be that some women would wish to be candidates for Parliament and some of us would be left out in the cold. I am hardly prepared to vote for that.

federal parliamentarian JAMES MCMULLEN in 1895, arguing against women's suffrage

I want for myself what I want for other women, absolute equality. After that is secured, then men and women can take turns at being angels.

AGNES MACPHAIL, federal MP from 1921 to 1940

The world has suffered long from too much masculinity and not enough humanity.

Alberta legislator NELLIE MCCLUNG

She might have had children of her own if she hadn't been too busy with other things.

Ottawa city councillor PAUL TARDIF, slighting longtime adversary Charlotte Whitton, who had never married. Upon becoming mayor in 1952, Whitton had got rid of the limousine and chauffeur that came with the job, saying, "I've never had a man or a Cadillac in my life."

Women have to be twice as smart as men to prove they're half as good. Fortunately, that's not hard to do.

Ottawa mayor CHARLOTTE WHITTON

Trust in God and she will deliver.

Ottawa mayor CHARLOTTE WHITTON

Speak up, gentlemen, I am not opposed to male participation in government.

Ottawa mayor CHARLOTTE WHITTON during a city council debate

Women make the best cooks and housewives and should be encouraged in that role.

B.C. politician WILLIAM VANDER ZALM in 1976

I suppose if three-toed bats were in vogue this year, he would have chosen one of those.

IONA CAMPAGNOLO, candidate for a B.C. seat in the House of Commons, in 1984, dismissing as opportunistic Walter Mondale's choice of a woman, Geraldine Ferraro, as his vice-presidential running mate in the 1984 U.S. general election

Down, girl!

Liberal leader JOHN TURNER on the campaign trail in 1984, admonishing an aggressive questioner among the reporters who accompanied him. A product of the old school, Turner was oblivious to the innovation of female journalists and persisted in addressing reporters as "the gentlemen of the press," "the boys," and "guys."

Just quiet down, baby.

Justice Minister JOHN CROSBIE in 1985, in Commons debate. The barb was directed at Opposition MP Sheila Copps. At the time, Crosbie was responsible for laws respecting the equality of women.

Woman's place is in the house, and that's where she should go just as soon as she leaves the office.

Liberal MP SHEILA COPPS in 1986

The whole organization should be eliminated. Its research is garbage. Why subsidize a lobby that slams our policies?

Tory MP BARBARA GREENE in 1989, condemning Canada's largest women's lobby (and vigorous opponent of many policies of Greene's party), the National Action Committee on the Status of Women (NAC)

It's the second F-word. It's a negative label.

Yukon MP and future NDP leader AUDREY MCLAUGHLIN in 1989, noting that the savviest female political aspirants shun the feminist label

Pass me the tequila, Sheila, and lie down and love me again.

Tory cabinet minister JOHN CROSBIE in 1990, referring to Liberal MP and future Liberal house leader Sheila Copps. Crosbie said her candidacy for leadership of the Liberal Party reminded him of an old song.

What a slut.

Tory MP WILLIAM KEMPLING of Ontario in 1991, attacking Liberal house leader Sheila Copps

Once you join the Commons fraternity, you begin to understand why there are so few women here. It isn't just the lack of money to finance their campaigns. It becomes apparent that women find less reward from trying to win elected office than from working in the advocacy groups that attempt to influence Parliament, groups that often are not only staffed mostly by women but headed by women. They watch the antics in Question Period, and conclude that party politics is a joke....The way to get more women into Parliament is to make it more relevant. We can only do that by getting rid of the adversary system, the unproductive partisanship, and the image of parliamentarians as useless ciphers. Watching the male-

dominated activities of Parliament, in contrast to the female-dominated groups working on poverty, child-care, and environmental issues, convinces you of something: that men parade, and women accomplish.

Liberal MP Paul Martin in 1992, explaining his decade-long effort to recruit more women as Liberal candidates for the House of Commons and wrest campaign funds from the party to better ensure their election

Say, fella, is that a prohibited weapon with a barrel length of less than eighteen inches, possession of which is grandfathered by those who satisfy the requirement of being a genuine gun collector on or before October 1992 in your pocket, or are you just glad to see me?

Justice Minister Kim Campbell in 1992, practising her stand-up comedy skills at a Vancouver fundraiser after steering gun-control legislation through the House of Commons

Is that a hammer in your pocket or are you just glad to see me?

Dianne Mirosh, Alberta minister in charge of women's issues, playing a sex kitten in a 1993 skit performed with a fellow (male) Tory cabinet minister before an audience of 1,600 party delegates, one of whom later admitted, "They just don't get it—I mean the 20th century."

If a woman did what Pierre Trudeau did, she'd be dead. I mean, I'd be slut of the world.

NDP leader AUDREY MCLAUGHLIN in 1993, commenting on her status as a single woman and how that would play in the media were she to become prime minister, in comparison to the media fawning over Pierre Trudeau's bachelor status before and after his tenure as sole occupant at 24 Sussex Drive

When men of substance have a disagreement, it's called an intellectual debate. When women of substance have a disagreement, it's called the equivalent of being a mud wrestler.

NDP leader AUDREY MCLAUGHLIN in 1992

Apparently, just about everybody who quits their job is being sexually harassed. We must have one hell of a lot of attractive people working. If this is the case I have to admit to you that I have never been sexually harassed....If I were, I would certainly want to make it known that I had been so favoured.

Fisheries Minister JOHN CROSBIE in 1993, defending proposed changes to the unemployment system, whereby people who quit jobs voluntarily won't get benefits, but those who can prove sexual harassment will. After being attacked for having made sexist remarks, Crosbie "clarified" them, insisting he was only making a joke about himself and condemning his principal attackers—three fellow MPs and the head of the National Action Committee on the Status of Women: "Make a speech," Crosbie complained, "in which you say something which can be jumped on and we'll hear from the four horsewomen of the Apocalypse how terrible it is, how shockingly you behaved, how you should be driven out of public life, how you should be garroted, how you should be hung, how you should be decapitated." In counterattack, one of the MPs, Dawn Black of the NDP, said, "Thought to be extinct, yet again the Crosbie-saurus has lumbered out of the tar sands to wreak havoc. Known to be callous, verbose, obsolete, and bumptious, untethered this creature meanders about causing harm to all that fall in its path."

We have to restore honesty in politics, and I know that they are even keener on that score than other members of Parliament.

Liberal leader JEAN CHRÉTIEN in 1993, pledging to triple the numbers of female Liberal MPs, saying more women mean more integrity in politics

I thought about running as a man, but I decided against it.

NDP leader AUDREY MCLAUGHLIN in 1992, explaining why she opted not to take on a more abrasive style in order to win her party's leadership

One of the first recommendations was that I do something about my teeth—they were too crooked. Another theme was that my eyebrows were too dark. Some people wanted me to change my hair. A lot of people didn't like my clothes.

AUDREY MCLAUGHLIN on the image consulting to which she was subjected after becoming NDP leader in 1989

I think that clearly, somebody who has a family—that they have to look after and bring up—has got a commitment to other people that have families, and I think it's part of why people can identify with Charest.

Ontario Tory MP TERRY CLIFFORD, a supporter of Jean Charest's Tory leadership bid, in 1993, in a remark perceived as a slight against Charest rival Kim Campbell, who is divorced from her first husband, separated from her second husband, and has no children. Clifford's own family affairs were the subject of scrutiny in 1989 when the RCMP investigated him and fellow Tory MP Bob Hicks for using public funds to employ each other's daughters. No charges were laid; the two men said they hadn't violated parliamentary rules because they hadn't hired members of their own families. Campbell campaign manager Ross Reid, a Newfoundland Tory MP, responded to Clifford's remarks by saying, "I think that is just the worst kind of crap I ever heard in my life." Another Campbell supporter, Tory MP Don Blenkarn of Ontario, added, "What is this? A woman can't belong? Unless you've got three kiddies you can't belong." (Charest is married to his high-school sweetheart and has three children.)

slogan *n.* Rallying cry of doubtful syntax and sincerity.

The Eyes of the World Are Upon Alberta.

campaign slogan of WILLIAM ABERHART's Social Credit party in the 1935 election that first brought the party to power

Credit Is the Bloodstream of the State!

Alberta premier WILLIAM ABERHART's slogan, explaining his proposal—rejected by Ottawa—to create a provincial currency and revive the Depression economy by pumping freshly printed money into it

Christ's Call Forward.

a 1930s campaign slogan of the Co-operative Commonwealth Federation (CCF), predecessor to the New Democratic Party

No Angel but a Good Mayor.

slogan of Ottawa mayoralty candidate CHARLOTTE WHITTON, whose antics included brandishing a cap gun at council meetings, bursting into song, and joining the spectators' gallery in order to heckle her fellow councillors

Let No One Throw Sand in the Gears!

slogan of hardware merchant turned premier W.A.C. (WACKY) BENNETT of British Columbia in the 1950s

Davis Will Make It Go.

slogan for WILLIAM DAVIS's first, and successful, campaign as Ontario premier, in 1971

The Land Is Strong.

re-election slogan of the federal Liberal Party under Pierre Trudeau in 1972, crafted, it would seem, by someone who had been out of the country for some time: the dollar was falling, and interest and jobless rates were rising. The election reduced Trudeau's majority government of 1968 to a slim minority.

Self Control, not State Control.

campaign slogan of IZZY ASPER, Manitoba Liberal leader, in his 1973 electoral contest against the NDP government

Coalition of Common Sense.

electoral rallying cry of GRANT DEVINE's Tories in Saskatchewan in the 1982 campaign that brought his party to power

The Who's Farewell Tour.

popular button among anti-Joe Clark delegates at the 1983 Tory leadership convention. The phrase is a take-off on the *Toronto Star*'s front-page headline the day after Clark was first selected leader in 1976, "Joe Who?"

Jobs, jobs, jobs!

BRIAN MULRONEY's rallying cry in his successful general-election campaign of 1984

Sodomy Forever.

a play on "Solidarity Forever," an anthem of trade unionists and socialist politicians. The revision, suggested by Social Credit cabinet minister DAVE PARKER of British Columbia as a theme song for the

Opposition New Democrats, was defended by Parker's boss, Premier William Vander Zalm, who dismissed demands for a retraction, saying, "[The legislature] is not necessarily always a polite place."

We Are Not Sheep.

campaign slogan of the Rhinoceros Party in 1988

Kim Is Cuddlier.

campaign slogan of KIM CAMPBELL, candidate for frosh president at the University of British Columbia in the 1960s. Left-wing columnist Stan Persky, one of Campbell's fellow student council members at UBC, recalled in a 1993 *Maclean's* article that "she looked like a straight right-winger....I thought, 'Oh God. Here's the ancient regime.'"

smash in the face *n.* A quick, down-and-dirty interview, usually one-on-one, between a reporter and politician, in which the reporter, steeped in research, challenges the victim to dispute accounts of his or her equivocation on policy, betrayal of friends from childhood to the present, covert philandering, and overt vacationing at the public expense—the aim being to distill the responses into an objective, balanced article to be filed the same day as the interview for a 6 p.m. deadline.

solidarity *n.* We must all hang together, and certain of you will be hanged if you cross the leader.

Now that the trained seals are silent....

GEORGE DREW, Tory leader of the Opposition, in 1956, mocking the unity of government members during a debate on the trans-Canada pipeline in the 1950s

A government member must vote like a wooden soldier.

PHILIP GIVENS, Toronto mayor and Liberal MP, complaining about the constraints of cabinet solidarity

As far as I can tell, the party has an old guard and a new guard, and it also has a left and right wing, so you've got the old-guard left and the new-guard right and so on through all kinds of permutations, with the same people sometimes changing groups on certain issues.

Liberal strategist KEITH DAVEY describes to Lester Pearson the state of the Liberal Party, of which he has just become leader

We want everybody inside the tent pissing out. We don't want people outside pissing in.

BRIAN MULRONEY soon after securing the Tory leadership in 1983, welcoming longtime foe and Quebec MP Roch LaSalle into the fold

Like a dog with a whole bunch of new puppies.

FRANK MCKENNA in 1987, asked how he felt on the night of his Liberal sweep of every single seat in the New Brunswick legislature. The comment drew widespread criticism. "I walked into caucus and they all started barking," McKenna recalled in a 1993 interview with journalist John Lownsbrough. "I was very naïve."

You can't spit in the prime minister's eye and expect a brilliant career.

Tory MP CHARLES COOK of British Columbia in 1992, on his decision to vote against his own government's proposed legislation to hold a referendum on the Charlottetown constitutional accord

stamina *n.* The axiom that staying in power requires staying power.

At night my spirit leaves me. But instead of wandering up the Nile, it does push-ups.

JOE CLARK campaigning to retain the Tory leadership in 1983, responding to a reporter who asked him where he got his stamina

You don't need brains for this job, just physical stamina.

AUDREY MCLAUGHLIN, hours before winning the leadership of the New Democratic party in 1989

You need the stamina of a water buffalo, the hide of a rhino, and the energy of a go-go dancer.

Alberta senator STANLEY WATERS in 1989 on the qualifications for his job

statesman *n.* A politician whose reputation survives his or her press clippings. In Harry Truman's view, "a politician who's been dead for ten or fifteen years."

A statesman is a man who can solve great problems which wouldn't exist if there were no statesmen.

JOHN DIEFENBAKER

If there are any statesmen here, they'd better resign. I want politicians!

Prime Minister JOHN DIEFENBAKER to his cabinet colleagues

stature gap *n.* The yawning chasm between voter expectations of graceful, decisive, and even-handed leadership and the shortcomings of politicians whose rhetoric arouses said expectations.

In this game you have to be a bit of a sonofabitch. Joe doesn't quite have it.

Liberal strategist JIM COUTTS, who tagged Joe Clark's image problem as "The Wimp Factor"

How boring is he? It's said that if he were going down for the third time, someone else's life would flash before his eyes.

a line that made the rounds of the Ontario Progressive Conservative Party in the mid-1980s to describe the personality of leadership contender DENNIS TIMBRELL

I do feel quite overwhelmed by it and a bit flabbergasted. Couldn't we call it Campbellrationality...or Campbell discernment?

Defence Minister KIM CAMPBELL in London, England, attending to her cabinet duties in the midst of her 1993 bid for the Tory leadership, trying to downplay the fascination of the British media with "Campbellmania"

study *v.* To defer indefinitely. Better to suffer criticism for inaction than for taking the wrong action.

We have never before had a government which qualified to be called the "we-are-looking-into-it" government. Now we have.

JOHN DIEFENBAKER in 1967, referring to the Liberal government of Lester Pearson

My boy, you may one day have some responsibility. I would just give you one bit of advice, to remember that in the course of human history far more has been accomplished for the

welfare and the progress of mankind in preventing bad actions than in doing good ones.

Prime Minister LESTER PEARSON, recalling a principle he credited to his mentor Mackenzie King

It is good that Mr. Trudeau did not consult the cabinet. It would probably have insisted on a study session followed by a task force followed by a white paper about which nothing would be done.

T.C. (TOMMY) DOUGLAS, leader of the NDP, in 1971, commenting on the surprise announcement of Pierre Trudeau and Margaret Sinclair's wedding plans

style *n.* The surest impediment to a politician's progress, hence their heavy investment in the thriving trade conducted by speech, wardrobe, and grooming consultants.

I'm a hugger. I'm a tactile politician. I'm slapping people all over the place.... That's my style.

Prime Minister JOHN TURNER campaigning in 1984, after television cameras caught him patting the behinds of two prominent Liberal women—party leader Iona Campagnolo and Quebec party vice-president Lise St-Martin-Tremblay. Campagnolo responded to the Turner touch by slapping his posterior, saying, "that's from woman-o to man-o"—a mild retort to Turner's description of himself as a "*mano a mano*" (Italian for hand-to-hand) politician.

The public is moved by mood more than logic, by instinct more than reason, and that is something that every politician must make use of or guard against.

JEAN CHRÉTIEN in his autobiography, *Straight from the Heart*, in 1985

The essence of leadership is making people feel good.

dictum of JEAN CHRÉTIEN

succession *n.* A changing of the guard, hailed with a fanfare of trumpets and followed by much confusion and infighting, duly chronicled by media tribunes who note with approval the absence of chaos and backstabbing during the victor's glorious campaign.

I was my own best successor but I decided not to succeed myself.

PIERRE TRUDEAU in 1984, announcing he would not lead his party into the next election

[We are] erecting a new standard of morality day by day in Canada.

Prime Minister BRIAN MULRONEY in 1985, announcing the creation of tougher conflict-of-interest guidelines for cabinet ministers after five of his ministers had been forced to step down over alleged ethics violations in the first year and a half of his government; two more would follow them out the door in the nine months following Mulroney's vow to clean house. Many of the government's image problems flowed from Mulroney's apparent failure to make good on his election promise of "a brand new dimension [to government appointments] of objectivity and representation and fairness for all Canadians." Within a year of exploiting John Turner's electoral weakness of having made eighteen patronage appointments on the eve of the 1984 vote (which Mulroney had labelled "vulgar...shameful, and scandalous"), Mulroney had made 1,280 such appointments, drawing heavily in his selection of worthies from the ranks of his school chums and associates in his law practice and his days in business.

By virtue of my genes.

KIM CAMPBELL, Vancouver school board chairman and future leader of the Progressive Conservative party, explains in a 1983 *Vancouver Sun* interview how she came to be gifted with an abundance of intellectual talents. William Vander Zalm, a sometime adversary with whom Campbell once vied for the B.C. Social Credit leadership, thought her gifts were mostly in the bloody-mindedness department, telling *Maclean's* in 1993, "There used to be a joke: 'If it isn't Kim's idea, it probably isn't any good.'"

Imagine, ten years of sparring across the aisle with [Liberal MP] Brian Tobin and I do not even get a gold Timex.

Prime Minister BRIAN MULRONEY in 1993, during his last appearance in the Commons as Tory leader. When Mulroney crafted the line earlier in the day, his intended target was Sheila Copps; he substituted Tobin's name after noticing she was not in the House when the time came for his farewell comments.

T

taxes *n.* Not to be used. See "investment," "contribution," "shared sacrifice," and especially "revenue enhancement."

The promises of yesterday are the taxes of today.

Liberal leader MACKENZIE KING in 1931

There's nothing more permanent than a temporary government building, unless it's a temporary tax.

1950s-era Liberal cabinet minister C.D. HOWE, who erected probably more government edifices than any other elected official in Canadian history

Hi, taxpayers!

trademark cheerful salutation of St. John's mayor DOROTHY WYATT, who used this greeting with apparent glee in frequent radio and television appearances during her tenure as mayor from 1963 to 1981

The country most comparable to us has sent us a clear message — don't have a GST at any price.

Australian prime minister PAUL KEATING campaigning for re-election in 1993, citing the unpopularity of Canada's new Goods and Services Tax, which Keating's chief rival proposed to implement if elected, as a reason that Keating should be returned to office

We sent some of our people to Canada to learn how not to do it. They did everything wrong, every single thing wrong.

Australian opposition leader JOHN HEWSON in 1993, defending his promise to implement a GST-style "revenue enhancer" if elected. Despite the unpopularity of his rival, incumbent prime minister Paul Keating, Hewson was defeated.

tubular, go *v.* To go down the tubes. An election campaign most commonly goes tubular when unflattering data (red meat) is thrown to the media by opponents, or the candidate makes a career-eliminating comment (q.v.).

U

universality *n.* The provision of social-assistance payments to all citizens, regardless of need; a concept described as a "sacred trust" by candidate Brian Mulroney in 1984, and effectively defunct—save for medicare—by the time he left office in 1993.

Does Pierre Trudeau need an indexed pension?

Tory leadership candidate KIM CAMPBELL in 1993, arguing that social programs be more precisely targeted at individuals in need. Trudeau would seem not to fit into that category, but, then again, as Campbell noted, perhaps he does, what with his "growing family." Campbell's off-the-cuff remark was in reference to the former prime minister's three children by his former wife, now Margaret Kemper, and young daughter by constitutional lawyer Deborah Coyne.

V

vision *n.* A shining idea with which to stir the people from their numbed indifference, imparted with principled conviction or shameless manipulation, as circumstances dictate.

There would be a new house and new people to choose from, and our aim should be to enlarge the bounds of our party so as to embrace every person desirous of being counted as a "progressive Conservative," and who will join in a series of measures to put an end to the corruption which has ruined the present Government and debauched all its followers.

JOHN A. MACDONALD in a call to arms to partisans in 1854

There are many [campaign strategy] alternatives:

(a) All-out attack. "Turn out the rascals."

(b) A combination of attack and mild alternative action (the traditional Opposition approach).

(c) A "promise" campaign consisting of many general vote-catching specifics directed at various groups.

(d) A single issue campaign (such as King's Constitutional issue or Walter Thompson's health insurance issue in Ontario).

(e) A positive platform along the line of the 22 points in Ontario in 1943.

(f) A "switch" campaign, starting with one of these and switching to another at a strategic time.

(g) A "goodwill" campaign based on the assumption that people will vote for us if we don't irritate them into voting against us.

a 1953 Tory strategy document, outlining various plans of attack for unseating the government of Louis St. Laurent, whose Liberal government was comfortably re-elected that year (quoted in Dalton Camp's 1970 memoir, *Gentlemen, Players & Politicians*)

W

waste *n.* Label attached by the Opposition to government spending which the Opposition calculates will meet with public disapproval.

What's a million? I daresay my Honourable friend could cut a million dollars from this amount—but a million dollars is not a very important matter.

attributed to Liberal cabinet minister C.D. Howe, defending his government's spending habits with a regrettably memorable outburst that would greatly assist in its defeat at the polls in 1957

wasteland *n.* An asylum for lost or obscure causes, commonly located in the Senate and the backbenches of the Commons, but also extending to certain political movements at certain times.

He had by then entered the Senate and I had entered the Conservative Party—different purgatories for similar heresies.

Tory strategist DALTON CAMP, recalling a meeting with Senator Chubby Power

welfare *n.* Misdirected funds better applied to business subsidies to enhance global competitiveness or further reduce the stubbornly high price of entrées in the parliamentary restaurant.

Why should we continually have to jump in and rescue the children and the wife because he went off somewhere else?

B.C. premier WILLIAM VANDER ZALM on the dubious idea of state enforcement of child-support payments

wife of *n.* The political spouse as stage prop.

Behind every successful man stands a surprised woman.

attributed to MARYON PEARSON, wife o
Prime Minister Lester Pearson

Yes, about twelve cups of coffee and eight doughnuts.

MARYON PEARSON, asked at the end of a long day of campaigning with her husband if the couple "had anything else to bring up"

We've lost everything. We even won our seat.

MARYON PEARSON, who did not enjoy public life, bemoaning how she and her husband would have to remain in the political sphere even though his party had lost the 1957 election

The big problem is to find suitable hats. I don't care for them all that much, but you have to wear them in politics.

MARYON PEARSON

Welcome to Liberace and to the Prime Minister.

sign outside a London, Ontario, hotel where Lester Pearson was making a 1965 appearance. After his wife Maryon joked to her husband, "Second fiddle to a piano player," the sign was changed to read, "Welcome to Mrs. Pearson and her husband."

I sometimes found myself surveying the table with loathing and irritation: what in the world can I possibly find to talk to these crows about?

MARGARET TRUDEAU, ex-wife of Prime Minister Pierre Trudeau, in her autobiography *Beyond Reason*, on the trials of making small talk with the wives of visiting male dignitaries

I guess the biggest shock to me was all these people saying you cannot have two strong people together—if the woman is strong, the man is weak. The reality is that to have a strong woman, you need a very strong man.

MAUREEN MCTEER, wife of Prime Minister Joe Clark, responding to late-1970s criticism over her decision to retain her maiden name after their marriage

Stop crapping all over my husband.

MAUREEN MCTEER, wife of Tory leader Joe Clark, to reporters critical of his stewardship

I do sinks, I do all that, absolutely....And my husband does a lot of things. Brian rinses out his tub, he certainly does. There's a certain knowledge that one day all this is going to be over and there's going to be him and me and we'll have a little apartment.

MILA MULRONEY in 1984. In 1993, a few weeks after the announcement of Brian Mulroney's stepping down from the Tory leadership, the Mulroneys purchased a multimillion-dollar house in Montreal.

I know my role and I know my limitations. What I do within those limitations, that's up to me. I have always been very accountable for everything I say.

MILA MULRONEY in 1986

Her judgement, which is partly based on gut, partly on intuition, partly on reflex, is remarkable. Absolutely remarkable. For people, for issues, for political solutions. Just amazing. It's a good thing people don't know how influential she is.

Prime Minister BRIAN MULRONEY, on the political role played by his wife Mila

Z

zealotry *n.* Services beyond, way beyond, the call of ill-defined duty.

Politics is made up of irrelevancies. Politicians, when they have nothing else to do, immobilize themselves and everyone near them, obsessed, like Spanish border guards, with the continuous assertion of their authority. It is a mechanism for self-preservation.

Tory strategist DALTON CAMP in his 1970 memoir, *Gentlemen, Players & Politicians*

Little of signal importance in the global scheme of things has ever been at issue, much less determined, as a result of the Canadian political process.

DALTON CAMP in *Gentlemen, Players & Politicians*

I recognize that since you talked me into my present insane course some five years ago, it is only just that you should share some of the delirium, but you have probably had more than your share during 1972. My own capacity for accepting madness is now virtually unlimited—after five years—and I may soon be ready for the ultimate—trying to run this country—which you have almost achieved for me.

Tory leader ROBERT STANFIELD in 1972, shortly after a general election in which he nearly toppled Pierre Trudeau's government, in a letter of thanks to confidant Finlay MacDonald

Index to Quoted Sources

F

G

H

J

K

L

M

N

O

P

R

S

T

U

V

W

Z